Praises for *Love Yourself Successful*:

"Feeling stuck? Author and business coach Katrina Sawa helps you to see exactly what's holding you back and shows you that freedom, wealth, and love are entirely within your grasp. By following her simple, innovative strategies, you will see how you can be truly successful in every aspect of your life." —*Loral Langemeier, CEO/ Founder of Live Out Loud, international speaker, money expert, and best-selling author of the* Millionaire Maker 3 *book series and* Put More Cash in Your Pocket. *LiveOut-Loud.com*

"*Love Yourself Successful* is a compassionate and much-needed guide for any woman who dares to be successful, happy, and of service to the world. Katrina weaves clearly-defined action steps and practices with heartfelt personal examples to help you move beyond your comfort zone and into a life of greater, richer possibility. Pick up this inspiring book and get to work!" —*Entrepreneur Mentor, Ali Brown, AliBrown.com*

"In *Love Yourself Successful*, author and business coach Katrina Sawa provides straightforward, proven methods to create lasting change. We learn how to change our confining beliefs that keep us small so we can enjoy abundance in our work, finances, and even our romantic relationships. This is a must-read for everyone who wants the freedom to design and manifest her greatest vision." —*Sandra Yancey, CEO and Founder eWomenNetwork.com*

Love Yourself Successful

A Woman's Step-by-Step Guide to Finally Taking Charge of Your Life and Designing the Business of Your Dreams!

Katrina Sawa

AUTHORITY
PUBLISHING

Love Yourself Successful: A Woman's Step-by-Step Guide to Finally Taking Charge of Your Life and Designing the Business of Your Dreams

By Katrina Sawa

1. BUSINESS & ECONOMICS / Entrepreneurship 2. BUSINESS & ECONOMICS / Small Business 3. BUSINESS & ECONOMICS / Women in Business
ISBN: 978-1-935953-38-8

Cover design by Cathy Davis, DavisCreative.com
Interior design by Stephanie Martindale
Heart tattoo © Uladzimir Hryshchanka | Dreamstime.com

Printed in the United States of America

Authority Publishing
11230 Gold Express Dr. #310-413
Gold River, CA 95670
800-877-1097
www.AuthorityPublishing.com

Contents

Acknowledgments

Kathy Bennett, my hairstylist, for multiple chats in the chair about this book, my love life, and my big business vision.

David Neagle, one of my mentors who showed me how to learn to love myself fully and to just BE, rather than always DO.

My mastermind buddies, Christine Kloser, Lisa and Lucho Crisalle, Maria Gamb, and Dr. Cindy Brown, for always cheering me on, telling me I can do anything I want, and never criticizing or judging me in any way.

My clients, for trusting in me to help them jumpstart their businesses.

My social media followers and friends for encouraging me at all hours of the day and night.

My friends and family for believing in me all along the way.

"If you're not living on the edge, you're taking up too much room."

≈ David Neagle

Introduction

Who is this book for?

Love Yourself Successful is designed for you, the woman entrepreneur or want-to-be entrepreneur who wants to find the formula for living a happy, love-filled life running a consistent six- or seven-figure revenue earning business.

And if you're already thinking, "A six- or seven-figure business, I just would hope to make mid-five figures," that's OK. But we'll change that thinking later. Trust me.

The reason I know that you can do this by reading this book is because I've done it. I've been an entrepreneur since 2002, when I told my last boss to F*** off. Oh, yes, I did, and it was awesome! I never looked back, and I had NO PLAN B.

The first three years of my business were built on an old way of thinking, an old business model. I used to trade hours for dollars in a typical consulting business model. I had some clients on retainer, and some just hired me when they needed me to take care of some of their marketing.

I'll tell you more about me and my story in just a little bit…

When I found this new way of doing business, however, more freedom came, more money came, and I also manifested the man of my dreams.

Now, six years after CHANGING EVERYTHING, I've discovered true happiness in life, great love for my business (and myself), and an abundance of wealth.

Now, *Love Yourself Successful* isn't about giving you the "magic pill." I'm talking about a true and proven business structure and invaluable mindset shifts that can take place in your life over a span of months or years, as they did in mine. You choose how long!

Yes, there was hard work and long hours, at first. But now, only a short time later, I am experiencing my ultimate love-filled, moneymaking life and business.

You see, I'm a very emotional being, and, as one of my mentors always says, "We are spiritual beings living inside a physical body." It was important for me to finally uncover who I really was and what I was meant to do on this Earth. I didn't just want to go through life as everyone else told me to or as many others I saw did: blindly working harder to achieve more.

I wanted to find a way to have my life look a little different. I believed "it will all work out in the end," the title of a chapter I wrote in a different book back at the beginning of my journey.

I wanted to be so completely head-over-heels in love with the man of my dreams, whom I had yet to find. I wanted to make (at that time) a simple six-figure income, where I could be content providing my services and living the lifestyle I dreamed of living.

Little did I know…I was thinking WAY TOO SMALL!

There was so much more out there that was possible; yes, even for little old me. But it wasn't until I started to believe that I deserved and could have the love, and the money too, that things began to happen.

I'll be sharing my story and experiences with you throughout this book because I think it's important for you to hear about the struggles I overcame, the opportunities and leaps of faith I took, and the decisions I made to get me where I am today.

My hope is that you will read this book with an open mind and an open heart. It is important for you to do this to have the kind of life-changing experience that I believe you will have.

I've learned these business and mindset strategies from some of the best teachers in the industry. These people have been where you are, and where I was, and are doing great things in their lives and businesses to help others achieve more, just like I want to do for you.

My goal is to inspire, motivate, and educate you on what else is possible and how to achieve it for yourself in order to be completely happy and successful.

Love Yourself Successful is a step-by-step guide to redesigning your life, and possibly your business, so you can have both love and money. It's not about one or the other; it's about achieving both for complete and utter success and happiness. (Plus a ton of other factors as well, see the chart below.)

I mention money here because it's obviously a huge part of becoming successful. But without the love part first, the big money would never have come for me.

I'll explain more about how they go together later in the book.

Why should you read this book?

Whether you're a stay-at-home mom, professional working woman, woman in transition, current female entrepreneur, or even a man in any position in life, this book will give you easy, how-to strategies to:

- Uncover your true greatness.
- Discover what's missing in your life and how to change it.
- Change the way you think about your desires in life and business.
- Update your beliefs on what truly is possible for you.
- Enable you to think and play bigger.

- 🌺 Motivate you to take action towards building the life and business of your dreams.

- 🌺 Design a plan to finally achieve the success that you know you are meant to have.

I want to help you take the "work" out of your business and make it more fun or help you to design a business that you enjoy waking up to every day.

I want you to be able to work less and make more doing exactly what makes you happy.

I want you to be able to transform the lives of the people you are meant to touch with your business by enabling you to discover your true, authentic self, your purpose and passions in life, and by doing it all while NOT worrying about money.

You'll walk away with many ideas, strategies, thoughts, and discoveries that allow you to:

- 🌺 Enjoy a better love life (and sex life).

- 🌺 Believe in yourself fully.

- 🌺 Trust in yourself and the Universe.

- 🌺 Love yourself, your business, and others unconditionally.

- 🌺 Experience an abundance of wealth and success.

- 🌺 Transform your business to fit your ideal lifestyle.

How will this book make you feel?

Think ahead for a moment to a time not that far away from where you are, completely head-over-heels in love with your partner, spouse, or significant other. Nothing can keep you apart. You finish each other's sentences. You do kind things for each other every day. You make love with more passion than you ever thought you had.

You are in love with yourself and fully accepting of all your strengths and weaknesses.

Now think also about your environment and your family. You are so excited to welcome the people you choose into your home. They love to listen to you. They enjoy spending time with you, and you with them. They support you fully with all your ideas and dreams. There are only positive forces in your life at this time, pushing you forward towards your biggest dreams and goals.

Now think about your business, the perfect business that allows you to be just who you are. Imagine a business where you do exactly what you're meant to do and work with exactly who you're meant to work with. This business allows you the freedom to choose when and how you will work while providing you with an abundant income.

This is not fiction. This CAN BE your reality if you choose to accept it.

I've done it. Hundreds of my friends, clients, and peers have done it, and we continue to excel each year beyond our greatest expectations—even in a down economy!

YOU CAN DO IT TOO.

You may just have never been shown HOW to do it, HOW to achieve such happiness and success.

This book is a step-by-step guide on how to pull you out of your FUNK and on with your FUTURE!

You do deserve more. You will get it if you read this book and really take the time to do the exercises.

Love Yourself Successful is about having four types of love in your life in order for the money, true success, and happiness to come to you.

The four types of love you need are:

1. Love for self.
2. Love with a significant other.
3. A love-filled environment.
4. Love for what you're doing.

Throughout this book, I'm going to be talking about all four types of love and how they relate to your ultimate success, more money, and complete happiness.

First, we're going to look at what else you need to be successful.

You need to know two things in order to become successful:

1. You need to know where you are now.
2. You need to know where you want to be.

Then at the end, if you want to totally transform your business, or start up a new one, I will show you how to get started doing that.

What to do now

It was important to me to give you as many tools and as much information as I could in order for you to grow through this process. My friends and peers all say I give way too much information with everything I do, but that's what makes me different. However, my publisher said that a 1,000 page book just wouldn't sell! I laughed.

Instead, I put together a private resource webpage for you that will support you while you're reading this book.

On this page, you can download free resources, templates, and documents. You can listen to audios and watch videos that pertain to this book and its content. You will also have access to an online community where you can interact with me, network with others who are reading this book, attend periodic free tele-classes and calls directly with me, and begin outlining your new Love and Money Business.

You will also get access to a group of highly motivated entrepreneurs called **The Love & Money Club**.

So before you read any further, simply go to: www. LoveYourselfSuccessful.com/bookresources and you can download a free audio recording of me talking about *Love Yourself Successful* plus many other resources.

I will be giving you suggestions for exercises throughout this book that you will want to go to this page to download or take action on.

Plus, from time to time, I hold tele-classes, webinars, and live events (some paid, some free) with expert guest speakers or myself covering various aspects of The Love & Money Business Model and how to become more successful in your business. You'll get access to those as well if you sign up for my email newsletter while you're there too. Many of the resources, however, do not require you to sign up in any way, so I do encourage you to go check out what's there, at least. Remember to go to www.LoveYourselfSuccessful.com/bookresources.

Now, you don't have to download the audios or any of the resources before, during, or even after you read this book if none of that interests you. It is there for those of you who wish to work through the process and take the necessary steps to truly transform your life and your business, sooner rather than later.

"If one advances confidently in the direction of his dreams, and endeavors to live the life he has imagined, he will meet with a success unexpected in common hours."

❧ Henry David Thoreau

Chapter 1

Step One—
Where Are You Now?

What's up with your life?

So, first things first: What does your current life look like and feel like?

Are you totally and completely happy with every aspect of your life?

If not, what's missing? What doesn't feel right? Where do you wish things were different?

I'm not trying to depress you here. Hopefully your life is going pretty well at this point. However, in my experience working with hundreds of entrepreneurs over the years, especially women, I've found that most are NOT completely happy.

So, are you completely happy and in love with your significant other, or are you settling in your relationship hoping it will get better, they will change, or it will work itself out?

Do you currently not have a significant other and either wish you did or are still hurting from a previous relationship?

I believe that having this kind of love in your life is crucial to anyone having complete success or happiness in life or business. This isn't to say that you can never be happy without a significant other. We're going to talk about love for yourself as well through this process, so hang tight.

However, your love life is definitely somewhere we want to focus. In fact, it could be the crucial element for you, like it was for me.

When I first left the corporate world and entered into entrepreneurship, I was married. I thought my husband at the time had an entrepreneurial spirit, since we had actually met doing door-to-door sales. I figured that, because he was willing to do that kind of outgoing, self-motivated type of sales, he would understand me wanting to run my own business and have more flexibility in life.

I found out quickly, though, that he had many more concerns for our financial security than I had anticipated.

You see, I always knew I would be an entrepreneur at some point in my life. I had that feeling from an early age. I just didn't know what I would be doing until the point when I actually quit my last job.

I had been seeing a business coach for a few months prior to leaving my job, because I still felt a bit confused as to what kind of business I would start. I had a few different ideas, but I wasn't totally sure about any of them. Looking back on it, I had some fears that crept in, too.

I was scared to choose the wrong type of business and fail at it or not make any money. I was unsure of my own abilities to some extent, as well, and how to position myself to potential prospects.

So, where are you in the process of becoming an entre-preneur? Are you already one and loving life? If so, great! But what's still missing? Is it the money, the six-, seven- or eight-figure income that you're still waiting to achieve?

Or are you just starting out and determined to make it work, but you aren't sure exactly HOW to do it the right way? Let me show you how to make less mistakes, spend less money up front, and discover your true passion and what you are meant to do on this planet.

There is a definite way to structure your business and your life to have it all. In my mind, having both love and money is the key to extreme happiness and success. Not only can you and your family then have whatever you desire, but you can also serve or contribute to countless more people in the process.

It's time for YOU

In a moment, I'm going to have you outline what you want your ultimate lifestyle to look like. I hope you design it around what you truly want, not just about what others around you want or think you should have.

You need to take care of YOU first. You know that, right? So, are you doing it?

You won't be any good to anyone around you—kids, significant other, clients, family—unless you take care of YOUR needs first.

I'm not just talking about a massage and facial once a month, either.

I'm talking about taking care of the inner you.

This means:

- ❦ Nurturing your thoughts and feelings.
- ❦ Expressing your passions and desires.
- ❦ Discovering your true, authentic self.
- ❦ Developing your inner wisdom, peace, and purpose.
- ❦ Allowing yourself to grow, feel, and be one with God in order to be of service to those you are meant to serve and inspire.

Now don't get freaked out by that last statement about God. I'm not trying to get religious on you here, but finding a connection to a higher source of some kind will help you on your journey to becoming who you need to be. So feel free to replace the word "God" with whatever being, spirit, or energy you feel comfortable calling it. Some people I know call it "the Universe."

This is what happened for me.

About a year and a half into my business transformation from the old model to the new one, I'd done all I could do to move the business forward. I'd implemented all the ideas and strategies that my mentors had suggested. I'd marketed the way I knew how to market, but the big money still wasn't coming to me.

I couldn't figure out why. I was very frustrated, as you can imagine. All the hard work, long hours, and money spent, but it was taking forever to get the income where I wanted it to be. Maybe you can relate?

I was in a business mastermind group at the time, which was basically a group of my friends and peers. They kept telling me to "stop doing more" and "just to be me." I didn't get it at first and began getting frustrated.

"What the heck did that mean?" I thought.

For months, I struggled with these thoughts of "just being" and what that meant. I was the "just do it" girl; my claim to fame was that I got things done. I was an implementer.

What I found out with some soul searching and many months of one-on-one coaching with my mentor was that I wasn't being my true, authentic self.

Instead, I was trying to be this person with this great business and talent. The only way I can describe it is that it was all on the outside.

There was something about me that I didn't want to let out.

YOU are the key to happiness

Through many months of coaching, self-development, and business conferences, I met more and more people who seemed to have this inner work stuff all figured out. They were great inspirations for me. I believe I manifested them in my life to help me learn how to bring out the real Kat. (My friends call me "Kat.")

During this time, my husband and I decided to call it quits. It was actually a pretty amicable split and mutual decision, luckily for me. I didn't have to go through a big, ugly divorce, like many of my friends had. My ex and I basically realized that we had gone down different paths in life and grown apart: he more into a corporate position where he enjoyed the security of a monthly paycheck, and me into the less stable, yet fascinating, world of entrepreneurship.

What we learned from the experience is that neither of us was happy anymore. We had lost the passion for each other as well and were basically just roommates toward the end. We decided that we both wanted to be happy and we deserved to be happy and in love again, but to do that we'd be better off apart.

As I said, luckily for me, this was mutual. We had no kids either, just Zeke and Kitty. He got Kitty, our big. fat. old cat, and I got Zeke, our beautiful, 115 pound German Shepherd. As you can tell, I feel like I got the better end of the deal.

Many of my clients and friends and their significant others don't see eye to eye. Some think about divorcing, others try to stay and hope things get better. Either way, divorce is not a fun thing, but if you're truly not happy and you and your significant other are truly on different life paths, then why suffer?

You don't have to do what "they" say and stay together for the kids or to give it another try. If you've tried and they've tried (or are unwilling to try), then consider what your life would be like on your own.

Getting divorced is one of the best things I did for myself. I became totally free the day I decided to leave—free from the negative pull that he had on my energy, and more.

Your environment and the people you hang around with every day or every week affect who you are being, what you think, and how you interact with everyone, including your clients.

Think about that for a minute.

Who do you see often, for example, who always drains your energy? They need you to listen to them, their problems, their drama, or the negative stories that come out of their mouths.

Who do you see who criticizes what you do? Who questions your business savvy? Who makes you feel uncomfortable when discussing your business goals or achievements?

If you have people in your life who do these things, talk down to you, or, even worse, tell you flat out, "You can't do it," or, "You will only fail," how do you think this is affecting your business, much less your self-confidence?

You have to find ways to protect your environment, yourself, your self-esteem, and your self-confidence. Without a hundred percent self-confidence, do you really believe you'll ever achieve your highest goals?

Probably not.

Lack of confidence in even the smallest or most insignificant way, a way in which you may not even notice, is one of the major reasons I see small businesses fail—or fail to launch.

Making the commitment

Now that you've discovered some things about yourself that you may not have been aware of before, it's time to commit to changing them.

I'm going to cover each of these areas more in depth throughout the book, but at this point you should make at least a small commitment to yourself now that you will be open to change.

You want to define what's most important to you and what your ultimate lifestyle looks like.

Then you want to identify what your true authentic self looks like, what you care about, what matters to you, and how you want to continue living your life each day.

If this doesn't look like the way you are currently living your life now, then make the decision to do some work to change this.

It is all right for you to put yourself first. It is okay for you to make changes towards making yourself a better person. This is not selfish. This is actually selfless, because when you are happier, you will be a much better person, which means you will be able to be a better wife, mother, and businessperson as a result.

But you first have to DECIDE to make a commitment to yourself to do whatever it takes.

Love Yourself Successful is designed to give you strategies and ideas to help you rearrange your life and your business so that you can have more love and more money.

But regardless of what I say here and what small steps or actions you may take, without complete commitment on your part, you may not fully succeed.

Taking action now

The only action I want you to take at this point is to make the decision to put yourself first from here forward. You'll hopefully take more action throughout the rest of the book as well, but for now, this is the first step.

Remember, I'm talking about putting yourself first in life in general.

Choose not to surround yourself with any negative forces, people, or events. (Stop listening to negative news and media stories too, if it helps!)

Listen to the inner voice inside you when it tells you to take time out or to treat yourself.

Allow yourself to satisfy your needs before the needs of others. Obviously except for emergencies or for your children, to some extent.

ACTION STEP

On the book resources page at **www.LoveYourself-Successful.com/bookresources**, there is a Love & Money Lifestyle Vision Board template that you can download now for free and use to map out the things you want to attract into your life. Just print it out and attach pictures, words, and phrases that fulfill you, make you happy, or represent goals you may have. Post your Vision Board on a wall in your office so you can see it every day to keep you motivated.

If you haven't listened to the free audio on that page yet, this would be a good time to do that. On it I share how to start believing in yourself and what it is that you want, as well as how to think bigger about what you could have.

If you have a journal or want to start a new one to journal your thoughts in while you read through this book, that could be a good exercise for you as well. Write out what you really want, who you really want to be, and if there are any negative things or people in your life right now getting in the way of having this.

Chapter 2

Step Two—
What Do You Really
Want?

Thinking bigger

All of us have goals in life.

Some of us have bigger dreams than others. Some have very small day-to-day desires.

Some write down their goals annually.

Some just keep them in the back of their minds.

What are your goals, and how well do you put them forth?

Do you just "hope" to make more money this year, or do you plan to make 30% more over last year's income? (Or more!)

You see, there's a difference in those ideas.

One is vaguer and pretty wishy-washy, in my mind.

The other is very specific and results-oriented.

Which do you think will actually come true?

Well, if the Universe doesn't know exactly how much more you want to make over last year, then how is it going to arrange to make sure you accomplish that? It may just send you a few extra thousand dollars. Is that enough?

Oh, I will talk about "the Universe" a lot throughout the book. To me, the Universe is what I call the higher being/source in which I believe. It's a "give to get" way of thinking. I believe that what you put out there with your thoughts or actions, you will receive back. You can see how being clearer and more precise with your goals would be helpful in this instance.

What are your goals?

Money goals, love goals, and life goals: These are what you want to set up every year, or month, if you prefer.

Money goals can include any of the following:

- Specific amounts of revenue you want to generate in your business
- Net profit you want to produce for yourself
- Certain percentage of income more than last year
- How much you plan to donate to charity
- How much you want to put into savings or reserve accounts
- What else you will invest in to increase your wealth

Love goals can include any or all of the following:

- Increase the amount to time you express love to others
- Increase your love and confidence in yourself
- Increase your self-worth or self-esteem
- Surround yourself with those who love you unconditionally at all times
- Surround yourself with those who support, inspire, and motivate you

- ❦ Spend more time with loved ones
- ❦ Create self-care rituals or routines
- ❦ Improve communication and passion with your current love or find the love of your life

Life goals could be similar to your values and can include any or all of the following:

- ❦ Find and buy a better house
- ❦ Treat yourself and your family to two or more week-long vacations a year
- ❦ Learn how to become a better person
- ❦ Help as many people as possible
- ❦ Give whenever you are called to give

Now once you write these down, I challenge you to think bigger.

Raise those money goals; triple them if you have to. You can do more, you can make more, and it doesn't have to be hard. You don't necessarily have to work harder to make more money, like your parents or grandparents used to believe and tell you. You don't have to know HOW it will happen, but if you can think of a higher number, write that down instead.

Get specific with your love and life goals. Put time-frames on them and goal dates that are sooner than you think will really happen.

This is not about what you think is possible now or what you could accomplish now; it's about what's truly possible once you decide to put yourself first and make some real changes in your life.

Stretching your comfort zone

This is where I want you to be...uncomfortable.

I want you to think so big that you can't even imagine accomplishing those goals right now, and you definitely have no idea how you'll get there.

Being uncomfortable is good. It means you're stretching beyond what's comfortable for you. This means you're going to achieve more, especially if you keep taking action steps toward what you want.

However, if at any point during this process of your life you get stuck and retreat to what's comfortable, what will happen?

You'll get stuck at where you are right now, right?

There is a statistic I like to quote that I heard a couple years ago, so it's probably a little outdated now, but I thought it was shocking:

> Only 5% of the US population is making over $100,000 per year and only 1% is making over $365,000 per year.

Why do you think that is?

I believe it's due to people reverting back to what's comfortable for them when things get a little tough or they aren't sure how or what to do next.

Instead, why wouldn't you ask for help and guidance then take inspired action?

So, are you ready not to be stuck anymore?

Are you committed to being a little uncomfortable for a while in order to get this fantastic new lifestyle and business that makes you so happy you could scream?

If so, keep reading.

If not, stop and pass this book on to a friend, sell it in a garage sale, or stick it on your shelf until you're ready.

One of the lessons I've learned is that there is no way I would have gotten where I have today, or where I will in the coming years, without being extremely uncomfortable along the way and with almost every decision, small or large.

Stepping out in faith

Faith is the word that has basically defined my actions over the last nine years.

I always knew that it would work out for me, becoming an entrepreneur. Going back to a J-O-B was not an option back then, and it's not an option now.

If you have it as an option now in your life, then I'd say you aren't serious enough yet.

If you have "getting a J-O-B" as Plan B in your life if this entrepreneur thing doesn't work out, then I'd say with about 99% surety that you will probably not succeed.

It may not be this year or even the next, but it will happen, most likely because you are not committed to making it work. Hang in there, though, because this book is designed to get this idea out of your head if you are truly meant to be an entrepreneur.

Now, this feeling that you need a Plan B in the first place could go away once you start taking action. If it does, then you have a chance. If not, you want to do more work on your mindset about needing an alternative if your business fails.

Many times, when we're not truly committed like this, it's due to one of three reasons, as one of my mentors always said: lack of love, self-esteem, or security.

It could be because of more than one of these.

For me, it was lack of love. Lack of love for myself to the extent that I was not being the type of woman that the potential man of my dreams would want. I had feelings of inadequacy that I was fat, not sexy, and not good enough in business.

I compared myself to my peers at times and still do to some extent.

I had a low self-worth issue. I later found out through a reading of my palms by a friend that low self-worth was my life lesson—the issue I was meant to deal with my entire life. Until I learned to accept this, the lesson was mine to learn. Once I became aware of it in my daily life, I could do things to help me push it aside.

Part of this has to do with self-esteem as well, so I guess I had a little lack of love and self-esteem both.

However, I never really had a lack of security. This is the feeling that there is a shortage of money. For some, security equals how much money one has, and for others it means basic needs, like shelter and food, as well.

I was always in a position in which I knew that if anything happened to me, my family members would help me out financially as they could afford to do so. (This isn't necessarily the case today, however.) So this wasn't a big issue for me growing up. I never felt like we had to go without or had any money issues in our family.

Many people grow up with those scarcity beliefs and fears because their parents said things like, "We can't afford that," or, "You can't have that because we don't have the money."

For the majority of people, however, security plays a big part in your overall belief system. Your mind can play big tricks on you, making you think things like, "I can't afford that," "We don't have the money for that," "That's not in our budget," or any other negative phrase that may be playing in your mind when any kind of opportunity appears. Typically these beliefs come from our parents or someone else when we were young. They get ingrained in our subconscious, which is the reason we do certain things and make certain decisions.

The steps you take in complete faith towards your goals and ultimate lifestyle that you want, regardless of all these feelings or emotions, are what will catapult you into the most successful, happy life that you can possibly imagine.

However, as I said before, the majority of people (95% of them, according to that statistic) don't take these leaps of faith; they revert back to what's comfortable.

Are you in the right career or the right business?

I'm only going to touch on this a little bit here because we first have to get you squared away in the love department.

However, about 20% of my coaching clients come to me because they're doing the wrong thing for their business or career.

They aren't always aware of this when we get started, but after close evaluation of what it is that they really want, they often discover they want more. They aren't happy doing whatever it is that they're doing or happy doing it the way that they've been doing it.

What I mean is that people come to me who work in a nine-to-five J-O-B and want to start a business, but they either aren't sure what to do that can replace their current income or they can't figure out how to make what they've started work to replace their income so they can quit. They are often somewhat willing to invest in their learning or invest in a business but often get sucked into a business model that isn't a good fit for them personally. They wonder why it's not bringing in enough money and why they're working so hard. All the while they're getting more frustrated and burned out with their J-O-B.

I'll get women who've started home-based businesses, but they treat them like a hobby, not a business. They don't have a business bank account. They built their own website. They're doing everything themselves. They're not investing any money basically in their own learning or marketing, then they wonder why they aren't making any money.

Then there are the women who come to me who have built up a pretty successful business; either they work from home or have an office. They may have employees or contractors, but usually not. They're usually working way too hard in the business trying to do it all themselves. These women also usually are in the old business model, not a more leveraged business model like the ones I do and teach. They just don't know what to do to increase their business and income from where it is now because they're already working too hard.

Do you possibly relate to one of these?

My point is that sometimes you just don't know what you don't know.

Before I learned how I could transform my own business into one with group coaching programs, tele-coaching with women all over the world, live events, online marketing, membership models to work less, serve more, and make more, I had no idea what I didn't know.

I had to invest in myself and my own learning to find out what it was I didn't know. Many people are not willing to do this, especially if they can't calculate the specific return on investment (R.O.I.). They also don't take action because they have that scarcity money mindset. They will just say no to opportunities out of habit.

What is important here is to figure out, if you can, how you would most like to spend your day working, with whom, and in what ways. You will learn more of what else is possible for you later in the book.

Designing your ultimate lifestyle

I realize I asked you previously to describe what you wanted your ultimate lifestyle to look like, but do you now have a slightly different picture?

If so, go back, revise it, and think bigger.

It's okay to have it all: the money, the love, and the complete happiness. If those around you don't believe it's possible or that you deserve it, then surround yourself with different people!

Realize and know deep down inside that it is okay for you to be happy, have all the money in the world that you want, and be more successful than anyone you know.

It doesn't mean that you're irresponsible or egotistical to want these things; in fact, it's natural. Too many people just settle in life.

- ☙ They settle for loving and living with someone whom they love enough or who loves them enough.

- ☙ They settle for a J-O-B that pays the bills, keeps a roof over their heads, and keeps food in their mouths or the mouths of their family.

- ☙ They settle for just getting by each month, knowing there's probably more they could have. But they don't know how to get there and aren't willing to try to find out how.

- ☙ They settle for thinking this is the life they've been dealt and that there's nothing they can do about it.

"They" are wrong.

I'm telling you that there is more out there for you. I've been where you are, thought what you thought, felt what you're feeling, and I found a way.

I found a way to be totally and completely happy in my life and with what I'm doing, to have love within myself and in my relationships, and to experience the money rolling in like never before.

I know hundreds of friends, clients, and peers who have also done this. But it takes work.

Mostly it takes work on the inside with your beliefs, your thoughts, and your decision to want more. The doing part is the easy part; I can show you that later. Seriously, though, if you're trying to boost your business and make more money, all the marketing in the world doesn't matter without the right mindset about love and money.

I encourage you to dig deep into your heart and soul to discover what you truly want in life and who you want to be.

ACTION STEP

Take out your vision board or write out a list of goals for yourself and think bigger. Journal about what else you want in life or what definitely needs to change for you to be completely happy. Think about and identify some of the stories going through your head that keep you playing small and where those might have come from. Write out how you feel about yourself. Do you love yourself fully at this point in time? Do you think you're beautiful, sexy, smart, and worth more? If not, what are you thinking that we need to address?

Make a list of the top three to five things you want to change about your life or your own thoughts that you will commit to working on while reading this book.

"If you want to be happy, set a goal that commands your thoughts, liberates your energy, and inspires your hopes."

❀ Andrew Carnegie

Chapter 3

Step Three—
The Love Factor

Why love comes before money

This is something that I learned the hard way.

After the divorce, I put everything I had into my business. I didn't pay very much attention to my own needs or love life.

I was running my business, doing all the right marketing, getting more exposure online and off, but the money just wasn't coming in very fast.

I didn't know what else to "do." I tried almost everything my mentors and peers told me, yet there seemed to be a missing ingredient to my success.

I see this with many of my coaching clients as well; they come to me for help to start, grow, or market their business or to give it a jumpstart. But I find out pretty quickly many of them aren't completely happy in their personal lives, in their relationships, or with themselves in general.

Rarely do I see many people succeed and reach big money goals in their business when issues in their personal lives like this are still apparent. Too many people, however, don't want to take the time to work on those relationships with others or themselves; they'd rather just dig their heads in the sand and focus solely on the business.

This hasn't been known to work, at least not for very long.

Why your success is dependent on love

You see, it's the love for yourself first and foremost that can catapult you over that next income hurdle.

Love for yourself = confidence

Love for yourself equals confidence, in my mind. How much of it you have depends on how well you sell, how much you charge, if you ask for the sale and how often, the feedback you receive, and so many other factors.

But without love and confidence or with a decreased level of it, how do you expect to truly reach your big money goals?

You probably won't.

So many women who come to me and work for themselves are undervaluing themselves in many ways; the biggest, most obvious way is by charging too little for your time. Women want to help others, and oftentimes you feel bad for charging for your time.

Oftentimes, you over-deliver, meaning you'll spend extra time with a customer or client. Even though they've only paid you for a specific amount of time, you'll go over the time they've paid.

Other times, if someone calls to just ask you a quick question, you may go ahead and answer it, letting them pick your brain, so to speak, all while interrupting your daily productivity flow. Instead, you can funnel them into a service or product that can help them, or better yet, not answer the phone at all. Scheduling a later time to talk will ensure you don't get pulled away from your immediate priorities.

Add up how many quick questions you've answered, and see how many billable hours that could have been over time.

So, love does come before money in many regards. One is you sometimes can't ask for more money unless you believe you're worth it. Knowing you're worth more comes from increased confidence and love for yourself.

Love + Money = Happiness & Success

The 4 types of love for success

Love Yourself Successful is about having four types of love in your life in order for the massive amounts of money to come in that you want and for the true success and happiness to be there.

1. Love for self
2. Love with a significant other
3. A love-filled environment
4. Love for what you're doing

I've already identified quite a few points around each of these types of love.

Where do you see that you have challenges in your Love Factor?

Do you have issues with loving yourself, loving and feeling loved by a significant other, having a toxic relationship, or valuing what you do and your worth?

Now is when we really dive in deeper, much deeper, into your thoughts, beliefs, and true desires.

ACTION STEP

This would be a good time to watch the videos that I have on the book resources page if you haven't already at **www.LoveYourselfSuccessful.com/bookresources**. Then journal more about how you want your life to look. What hours do you really want to spend working and when do you want to spend time with family and other responsibilities?

Chapter 4

Step Four—
Love For Self

Love comes from within

It was about two years into my business transformation. I'd already spent over $50,000 on coaching programs and mentors, yet I was barely making $70,000 in my business annually.

I decided to invest in yet one more mentor, but this time for a different reason, not for helping me figure out what to "do," but how to "be."

Notice that this new mentor was not in my budget. Too many of you think you have a budget, when in fact you probably don't. Maybe you should have a budget for self-learning and investing in your business, but even if you do, my experience is that whatever amount you think you should allot will never be enough.

With budgets, you have to also always be open to taking advantage of opportunities or people when they drop into your lap, like this next mentor of mine did, regardless of whether or not it's "in the budget."

It was an interesting part of my journey, to say the least. That year I grew so much, and I learned so much about myself. Basically, I cried through the whole year.

I learned to truly and deeply love myself for who I was regardless of what size clothes I wore, who I was friends with, how successful my business was, and whatever head trash popped into my head on a regular basis.

I used to compare myself daily with other mentors and peers who did similar things in business. I'd see what they would do, how much money it looked like they were making, the friends and status that they acquired, and I was darn right frustrated because I knew I had so much more to offer clients than they did, yet people were signing up with them left and right.

Hopefully, you can't relate to this. Yes, I'm a bit ashamed to admit it: I was envious of others pretty often.

When I learned to love my body the way it was, the personality I was given, I also learned to love and acknowledge the expert that I in fact was.

I was the best-kept secret in my industry! That's a joke I have with another mentor of mine; being the best-kept secret in your industry is not a good thing, by the way. You want to learn how to market yourself and get well-deserved exposure to become the recognized success you're meant to be. I'll get to that later, I promise.

The "ḦOT" Factor

Do you think you're "Hot?"

Yes, I do mean sexy, powerful, gorgeous, beautiful, and whatever other adjective you want to insert in there.

You need to think you're hot!

This matters in the case of love for yourself because you will instantly be more confident.

It matters when it comes to attracting the man of your dreams or re-igniting the relationship you've got!

It matters when it comes to your business, too, because that kind of attitude will make people want what you've got. I'm not suggesting you dress overly sexy; you can still be feminine, though, and feel hot in your business.

So if you do feel hot today, now, in your skin, then that's awesome!

If not, what's standing in your way of that feeling? What negative thoughts are rolling around in your head, preventing you from thinking you're hot? I call it head trash.

Having complete faith

We talked about having confidence, and how much you have of that will determine what you charge, offer, sell, and more.

Having faith is different. Having complete faith means you don't have a PLAN B.

- It means you will leap first, and then ask questions.
- It's about taking inspired action, going with your gut or intuition when you're called to do something.
- It means you don't look in your checkbook before deciding to invest in something; you decide to do it and then figure out how to afford it.

- ❧ It means you know whichever direction you go, you will land on your two feet; it will work itself out in the end.

- ❧ It means you never have to worry about money, because the Universe will provide just what you need, plus more.

- ❧ It means you take that inspired action without usually knowing HOW something will happen or what the outcome will be.

One of my mentors once gave me the example of a trapeze artist and what she has to do every day in her profession.

She has to leap from one trapeze to another, up high in the air, sometimes even without a net.

She has to let go of one trapeze before she can catch the next one. Usually she isn't able to reach both at the same time.

She has to have faith that the second trapeze will be there right when she needs it or she could fall to her death. She does this over and over again every day.

Oftentimes, in your life or your business, you have to make a decision or step out into something new, and you're between the trapezes, hoping that second one will be there for you, so you don't fall.

But, if you never let go of the first trapeze, what will happen? That's right, nothing; you'll stay right where you are.

I think about that story all the time when I'm making a big decision about something and I may not know what the outcome will be.

Do you have complete faith in yourself?

Complete faith that you will succeed in business?

How about complete faith that the relationship you're in right now is the right one for you?

If not, then let's work on that.

About three years ago, I was preparing the PowerPoint presentation for a speaking gig I had.

I was starting to outline the first few points about my journey, my story, myself, and the lessons I've learned along the way.

It was at this time I realized that one of the biggest reasons I was so successful building my business, attracting new clients, and great business-building opportunities was that I had complete and utter faith in myself.

I started thinking about all my clients and my friends and whether they had complete faith. Most of them didn't seem to have that kind of faith.

Yet I did. "How did I get that?" I began to think.

Was I born with it? Did my parents instill so much belief in me that I could do anything?

I wondered for a while and then just realized I was different than so many others.

I found in working with my female clients that rarely did they have this complete faith. They might have some faith, but not enough to just take big leaps of action towards what they wanted, like I did.

I had to figure out a way to help them increase their faith in themselves, their abilities, and their expertise and have them realize that it will all work out in the end for them if they just believe it will and take inspired action.

I had to convince them that they were experts. I had to, at the very minimum, get them to believe in my belief in them until they believed fully in themselves.

One thing I do with the clients who are coaches, consultants, or in some other service-related field is to tell them: "All you have to do is know more than your clients. As long as they feel like you can help them with whatever issue they have, and they see the value in hiring you, then you're the expert."

This can apply to anyone in just about any industry. You just have to know more about whatever it is that you're selling or doing than the person you're selling it to knows.

You don't have to know more than the person you perceive in your industry to be the leader; your customers will buy from you because they like, trust, and connect with you. If you show them your value, and that you can solve their problem, then you are the expert.

That will help you increase your faith, because this belief in oneself is something that actually will stop you from even starting your own business. Many people don't even get started.

Then once you start seeing the positive results from your inspired actions, your confidence and faith will increase even more.

Believing in the Universe

Ever since I was young, I believed in karma. If you did bad things, then bad things would happen to you. What goes around comes around.

I hadn't thought too much about the opposite until I started doing mindset coaching, which was even before *The Secret* was released.

The Law of Attraction has become very popular. However, it has its flaws, just as any other theory.

I don't believe it's just about thinking positive thoughts, doing affirmations, and sitting around waiting for the Universe to bring you what you want.

Many people think that sitting on their couch doing affirmations and speaking in the future tense about how they are now enjoying their million-dollar business in their new home with their great life are wasting their time unless they get up and take some action towards getting them there.

I believe that you do want to do the positive thinking part. In fact, you want to be very specific about what you want when you announce it to the Universe, either verbally, in a journal, or whatnot, because, otherwise, you may not get exactly what you expected.

I also believe that there has to be some doing.

No matter what your belief in karma, the Universe, God, or some other higher power, I think it's important to think, speak, and act in positive, meaningful, and results-oriented ways.

Keep your big love and money vision on top of your mind at all times so you are always focused on the big picture of where you're going.

One time, I was getting a reading by a psychic; this was when I couldn't figure out why the big money wasn't coming in faster. The psychic asked me a bunch of questions and did her little thing, then she told me:

"You're like a trombone. One day you're telling the Universe about your big vision, big plans, and you're very clear, and another day you're worried, scared, and acting like you don't know what you really want. The Universe doesn't know what to bring your way; you're up and down too much."

That was a big wake up call for me. I still think about that all the time. I tell that story to my clients, whom I see doing the same thing I did.

If you resonate with this, then keep this story in the front of your mind as well, so when you find yourself wavering on what you want, you can stop and remind yourself to focus on your big vision.

You DO deserve it!

Do you already know that you deserve complete happiness and success? If so, that's fantastic really, but consider yourself the exception.

So many women in general, whether they run their own business or not, believe what they have is what they've been dealt.

They stick with an unsupportive, unloving, or even abusive husband because they think they need to for the kids or because they took vows.

They continue banging their head against the wall in their J-O-B or their current business model because that's what they chose and have been doing for X number of years.

They don't ask for more help or invest in the next thing because they're still trying to figure out how to make the last investment work. Or their husbands tell them things like, "You can't spend more money in your business until you make the money back from the last investment." I hear that excuse a lot.

Sometimes you will make bad decisions—decisions and investments that don't work out or are a waste of money. You can't sit there and whine about it. Just chalk it up to a bad investment, set it aside, and move on.

Do you know how many times I've done this?

I've gone to numerous business conferences and events, many with the multi-speaker lineup (you know the ones). When I was first changing up my business from the old model to the newer, more leveraged model, I would invest in a ton of products, binders, CDs, and programs. Most of them are still sitting untouched on my bookshelves to this day.

The lesson I learned was that I wasn't a product learner; I needed to learn in person or from the horse's mouth, so to speak. I've got about $10,000 worth of bad investments sitting around, but I'm not complaining about it. Now I just never make those kinds of investments.

So, why does this relate to why you deserve success?

Because some people never even invest in themselves, their learning, their self-development, or their business in the first place. And the right learning will play a big part in your success.

You want to be open to new ideas, new modalities, new technologies, and new strategies.

How else do you think this practical get-er-done girl from the country ended up getting her palms read and seeing a psychic? It took me a couple years to warm up to these ideas of learning about myself, but once I started loving myself more, I increased the knowing that I deserved whatever I want. Then I opened up more on ways the knowledge and learning could come to me.

In order to become the success you know you're meant to be, you must believe you deserve it. You have to stop listening to anything and anyone who tells you otherwise.

ACTION STEP

Where do you see in your life that you could be settling or not taking action on what you really want? Do you fully believe in yourself, your abilities, and your expertise? If not, think about or journal about what you think has been holding you back. Write out three to ten adjectives that describe you as you see yourself today.

What are you telling the Universe it is that you want? Are you being consistent?

If you haven't listened to the free audios on the website yet, go do yourself a favor and listen. It could really open up your eyes about what's going on with you. Remember, you can go to **www.Love YourselfSuccessful.com/bookresources** for audios, downloads, and more!

Chapter 5

Step Five—
Love With a
Significant Other

Entrepreneur vs. non-entrepreneur mindsets

First, I want to bring up a very important factor: When in a love relationship or looking for your next Mr. Right, you want to consider what it takes to communicate between an entrepreneur and a non-entrepreneur. This is more common of a partnership than you may think.

If you're married to an entrepreneur, and you are an entrepreneur, then you could be OK here, although you may butt heads sometimes. But if you're an entrepreneur and he's not—he's an engineer (the furthest thing from an entrepreneur, by the way) or an accountant, corporate CEO, or employee—then you really have some work to do.

Entrepreneurial thinking is quite different from how salaried people think; you probably realize that by now if you're the entrepreneur. You think differently, make decisions differently, and are just overall different.

However, not a lot of couples actually discuss their differences in thinking, visioning, decision-making, investing, and having faith, etc. when they either get into business together or they get married in the first place.

Instead, couples in these types of opposite relationships tend to bump heads a lot in discussions about taking inspired action and which actions to take. The non-entrepreneur usually wants to take the more conservative, secure route knowing the outcome, while the entrepreneur usually wants to take the daring leap of faith with an unknown outcome.

Now, neither of these perspectives is wrong or right. However, if you want to get anywhere in your relationship or your business, and you're in this type of situation, you'll want to make a very big effort to get your communication on the same page.

Many people ignore their significant other's thoughts or concerns because it requires too much work to explain. Some of my clients have told me they've just not told their husbands about investing in coaching with me, someone else, or other business-building programs to avoid fights or them saying no.

Watch for this type of scenario, however. Does it feel like you're being supported when your significant other tells you no?

On the other hand, you don't really want to go behind your significant other's back either. That's a recipe for disaster, in my mind.

I think it makes more sense to find a way to discuss the topic—any topic. But you may have to get some help to be able to do this effectively, because oftentimes, unfortunately, the person we listen to the least is our significant other. If that's the case, you want to bring in a third party, another entrepreneur perhaps, or even a therapist. You want the counsel of someone who can see both sides of the issue and explain the differences in the two thinking styles and mindsets in such a way that it's not offensive or discriminating to either party.

If you ignore this, however, you may not find success. It could lead you to a big blow up and, possibly, divorce or financial devastation.

If you're an entrepreneur, single, and looking for your Mr. Right, like I am, then you want to make sure to put special notes in your "list" (of course we have a list) for what kind of personality you want your man to have. You can even be so specific to ask for another true entrepreneur; I'm becoming more and more convinced that this is what I need as well!

Another thing to consider is how much money you make versus how much he makes. On my dating quest this time around, I've only met one or two men who have seemed to make more money than me. Most men in the dating scene or online don't seem to be making that much money.

This isn't a problem for me, of course. I don't need a man to make more than me, or even to make a six-figure income, for that matter. But that has to not be a problem for him. In my experience, it is sometimes a problem for the man if he knows you make more money than he does. Therefore, now I'm more careful about specifically what I ask for from the Universe in regards to what kind of man I want to attract.

What's missing here?

What's missing in your life in regards to a love relationship?

Do you really have this now? Are you head over heels in love, and everything is peaches and cream between you and your significant other? Really?

Do you want or need more passionate love (or sex!) in your life, either with your current significant other or your ideal mate?

Are you not sure how to get it?

Are you wondering if the person you're with will ever come around and support you?

Are you wondering if your Mr. Right is out there or if you should just settle with someone who's good enough?

Are you afraid to ask for what you really want because he may not be out there?

Are you unsure of what to ask for?

Or do you have "a man is not a plan" syndrome, in total denial that being in love means anything to you or your success?

Maybe you just got out of a tough breakup, and you're nowhere near jumping back into one yet; OK, I understand that.

I just want you to identify what's missing regarding your love life.

I know that when I was married, what was missing for me was intimacy. We had gotten to a point where there was no kissing, hugging, holding, cuddling, or loving sex, either. That was so hard for me. I am such an affectionate, emotional woman; I was crying out for attention and love for two years before I finally realized that was no way to live, and I called it quits.

And a few years after my divorce, I was ready to find my Mr. Right (again). I had "a great big hole in my heart," is how I described it. I was happy with myself, my business, my income, my friends, and my support structure, but the one thing that was missing was that deep, passionate love for and with a significant other who felt exactly the same way.

Not that you "need" a man, don't get me wrong, but for many of us, we need that "love relationship" in our life no matter how independent and outgoing we may be. I know I do, and I'm a very strong, independent, outgoing woman.

Think about it, and think about what you truly want deep down inside, not just what you have experienced in the past or what you have currently.

What do you really want?

What did happen pretty early on that year of working a lot on myself, self-love, and mindset is that I became very clear on the type of man I wanted in my life. Unfortunately, back to the list, I left off two crucial, key characteristics, and the relationship I attracted at that time didn't end up being my happily ever after.

But I learned that I needed to change the way I was being in order to attract him. I needed to be more open, loving, and feminine overall in my day-to-day activities, not just when out on a date.

As a very outgoing, independent entrepreneur, I tend to exude a very strong and confident attitude in my business. This, for many men, comes off as masculine energy. And to a really confident, outgoing, successful man, like the one I want, he isn't typically attracted to that type of energy.

So feminizing up my overall demeanor was something I took on as a challenge to do. (There I went again with the "doing" right!)

Once I made the decision to do this and I changed my perception about how I was being to attract the man of my dreams, it happened pretty quickly; within six weeks I met him. We fell in love in just a few months and my whole world changed.

Now the ending to that story isn't as happy as you'd think. Unfortunately, it ended up not working out after two years; he broke my heart.

But the good news is that I still love myself, more than ever, in fact. I'm even more clear on what I want, who I want to be with, and that I'm not going to settle until I find the perfect man and relationship for me. I know he's out there.

Are you settling?

Every year for the past three years, I've held a live event called The Love & Money Business Summit. Last year I added a second event called the JumpStart Your Biz "in a Weekend" Intensive. Now I currently hold them both every year.

When I initially began planning The Love & Money Business Summit the first year, so many things started coming to me; that is actually what sparked me to write this book. The more I was in love, the more everyone around me needed to be in love, too; it was just such a great feeling.

At that event, though, I had attracted a few women, at least four, who were unhappy in their marriages. They came to the event that year to learn business and marketing strategies to jumpstart their businesses, but they also subconsciously came because of the Love Factor. I know this because we've had discussions about it back then and since then.

What those women experienced at that event with me was so uplifting for them. They finally became aware and acknowledged the fact that they deserved to be happy, they deserved to have love in their lives, and they deserved to be supported. They all decided to go home and have some deep conversations with their husbands; two were ready to leave them and one did leave. The other stayed because her husband came around and started making an effort.

They asserted themselves in their relationships, some for the very first time in their lives.

The end result now, two years later, is that all of them are happier. No one died. No one became homeless, ran out of money, or anything horrible like that. They all survived, and are now thriving, happy, successful businesswomen.

All of them had kids, and they realized that if they weren't happy, what kind of example were they sending to their kids? Yes, divorce is hard for everyone involved, including the kids, but most people are much better off out of a toxic relationship or environment than in one.

So, I encourage you to think long and hard to see if you're settling for anything you don't need to be. Examine if there are any possible actions you can take to get yourself and your kids into a happier, more loving environment or to fix the one you've got. It's so worth it.

Giving and receiving more love

Another subject I like to discuss in my live events and in my Love & Money Home Study System, as well, is the book *The 5 Love Languages.*

The 5 Love Languages is a book by Gary Chapman. If you haven't read it, it's a must read, whether you're married, single, or divorced.

I like this book because it is so straightforward and easy to read. In fact, the man I met who broke my heart and I read it together when we first started dating… Funny, huh? Too bad we didn't continue reading it month after month throughout the relationship! (I highly recommend doing something like that in your relationship. I know I plan to with the next man, for sure.)

Just like you learn effective communication strategies in business and how to talk to your customers and prospects and model their ways of learning, you want to learn effective communication for your relationships, too.

In *The 5 Love Languages*, Chapman talks about how to express heartfelt commitment to your mate. The way you like to receive or give love to or from your mate could be completely different than the way he likes to receive it or give it to you.

The 5 Love Languages are:

1. Words of Affirmation—For those of us who have this love language, we prefer to receive compliments, acknowledgement, appreciation, encouragement, empathy, kind words, and requests instead of demands.

2. Quality Time—For those of us who have this love language, we prefer to spend undivided and undistracted attention with our mate. That means no multi-tasking or interrupting and quality listening and conversation rather than problem solving.

3. Receiving Gifts—For those of us who have this love language, we prefer receiving physical symbols of expression and love. The cost doesn't matter; it's the thought that counts. Giving the gift of self is good, too. We definitely don't need it to be a special holiday or have a reason; any gift anytime is thoughtful.

4. Acts of Service—For those of us who have this love language, we prefer you show your love by performing small or large acts of service. That doesn't mean being told what to do, but doing things around the house, or whenever, just because you know it will make us happy.

5. Physical Touch—For those of us who have this love language, we prefer more kissing, hugging, holding hands, and definitely more intimacy and sex. Physical touch can make or break a relationship. It can communicate hate or love.

What is your love language(s)? You could have more than one.

Here are three questions to ask yourself to find out:

1. What does your significant other do or fail to do that hurts you most deeply? (The opposite of this could be your Love Language.)

2. What have you most often requested of your significant other? (That thing is probably what would make you feel most loved.)

3.   In what way do you regularly express love to your significant other? (What you do could indicate what you prefer.)

Another one of my favorite relationship book authors is John Gray, who wrote the *Men Are from Mars* series. If you aren't familiar with his books (he has a ton), and you want to improve the communication or passion in your relationship, you should read his books, too.

Love is a choice you make every day. Your self-worth often depends on if you are loved enough. Your business success depends on your self-worth.

If you want more love, you have to give it to yourself first, then to others. If the ones you want to love you can't reciprocate, or won't work on finding out how to fulfill your love needs, then you have to think about what you want your life to look like moving forward and make a decision to stay and settle or move on and thrive.

Relationship Rescue

It's obvious that communication is the key to building or rebuilding any new, or existing, relationship.

However, both parties need to want to make it work if it's going to work.

Both parties need to make an effort if it's going to work, as well; wanting is not enough.

Through my numerous coaching calls with clients experiencing many of these relationship issues, I developed a list of 6 Relationship Rescue types of activities to help you. These can be good for those in a relationship now, or even in dating situations, if you're single.

6 Relationship Rescue Activities:

1. Communicate the importance of discovering each other's needs, desires, concerns, dreams, passions, motivation level, and love languages.

2. Invite him to have a discussion about your future and the big picture, goals, passions, desires, wants, needs, and sex too. Explain the importance of him learning more about your business, or at least understanding more about why it is you're doing what you're doing, listening to your big vision for your business. Help him understand it if he's a non-entrepreneur.

3. See if you're both on the same page or identify where there are gaps in your thinking, devotion, and motivation.

4. Show your support, respect, love, and understanding for his points of view.

5. Agree on and set boundaries, time for learning, alone time, together time, money talks, love, sex, and other lifestyle dynamics.

6. Grow together when at all possible, attending self-development, spiritual and/or business events together, listening to tele-classes, reading books, and having regularly-scheduled partner meetings of some kind.

A special disclaimer: I'm not a therapist or relationship counselor of any kind, just a really observant and intuitive woman entrepreneur who's seen thousands of women in these situations.

If you're on the verge of divorce now, or you're extremely unhappy and thinking about it, and you want to try repair the relationship first, here is my seven-step action plan for working it out that you can try:

1. Make a list of everything you LOVE about your significant other. (Or WANT in one, if you're looking!)

2. Tell him what these things you love are. (Do this maybe after date two or three, or if you're ballsy like me, put it in your online profile to weed the wrong guys out from the start.)

3. Invite them to have a discussion about your future together and each of your big picture goals, passions, desires, wants, needs, intimacy expectations, and love languages too. (Do this maybe after date five or six, if you're single.)

4. See if you're both on the same page, or identify where compromise needs to happen. Talk about what a compromise would look like. (Identify and discuss red flags with whoever gets to date seven.)

5. Develop an action plan together and agree upon what changes need to happen and expectations or boundaries need to be set in place in order to move forward (either way).

6. Listen intently, support unconditionally, and don't judge.

7. Be seen, validated, and heard; don't hide in the background or you'll never get what you really want.

And for those of you who know there's no hope, here is my five-step action plan for letting go:

1. Make a firm decision.

2. Believe in yourself. You deserve more.

3. Protect your interests (financial, emotional, children, etc.)

4. Surround yourself with support (a must!)

5. Take charge of your new life and go BIG!

ACTION STEP

Identify where, if anywhere, you are settling in your personal relationships. Is it with who you're with now or who you hope to find? Make a decision about what you want in your love relationship and take steps towards getting it—stay and work it out, let go and move on, or build the list of what you want if you're in the same boat as me in finding the man of your dreams.

"What counts in making a happy marriage is not so much how compatible you are, but how you deal with incompatibility."

※ Leo Tolstoy

Chapter 6

Step Six— A Love-Filled Environment

Your support system

When we think about a support system, we typically think of our significant other, if we have one, friends, and close family members, right?

Well, those actually haven't been the biggest part of my support system, or that of many of my peers and friends in their own businesses, either. It's not because they aren't supportive or don't love us, but it's usually because those closest to us don't understand what we're doing. Unless they're in business for themselves too, they may not get you. Usually the people who do get you are those peers, friends, or close business professionals who are in the day-to-day grind with you who understand us the most.

For me, the best supportive people in my life are true typical entrepreneurs just like me. They get my frustrations, my creative ideas, and my zany, brainy marketing schemes. They understand why I invest thousands of dollars to fly across the country for a four-day workshop.

It's the ones closest to us who often don't really understand us, and, therefore, can't supply us with the unwavering level of constant support that we need to succeed.

It's not that they don't love us. In most cases, they very much do. That's why they may warn us, criticize our ideas, or doubt our abilities; it's out of fear and concern that we don't end up hurt in some way.

Many small business owners try selling to friends and family members first. In fact, network marketing companies suggest you go to them first.

In my experience, my friends and family are some of the last people who would pay for my advice, coaching, and products if they wanted to start, grow, or market their own business.

I do have some exceptions to that rule in my family, however; my cousin paid to attend one of my Love & Money Business Summit events once, and my uncle once had me come in and consult with one of his business partners, too. I even helped my mom get a blog and email newsletter started so she could maximize her jewelry business.

That's the extent of it, however. I have numerous close friends with their own businesses, not necessarily doing what they really should be doing. After years of them switching around from job to job or business to business, they still haven't asked for my help. I think they just don't understand what it is that I do and how I can help them.

They are all, for the most part, pretty supportive. My mom and my aunt both read my email newsletter; shoot, that's how they know what I'm doing, since sometimes I'm too busy to call!

For the most part, however, the bulk of my support system includes friends I've met through other mentors, in mastermind programs, and at events around the country. They are the ones I call and cry to when I'm having a bad day or celebrate with when I've made a big sale. They are the ones I email for advice on a product, service, sales page, problem, or concern. They do the same to me.

No matter whom you chose to be your steady support system, just make sure they get you. They need to listen to your big ideas without bringing you down, lift you up, and be your cheerleaders when you need them. And if the people in your support system change over time, that's fine too; the more support the merrier.

Toxic relationships

How you feel and are treated in your personal life reflects how you project yourself in your business, and that ultimately determines your level of success.

Toxic relationships are the ones you have to watch out for; these are the ones that consciously, or subconsciously, can sabotage your success.

If any of the following scenarios apply to you in any way, you could be in a toxic relationship.

- Someone you love or respect (these are the naysayers) tells you:
    - "You're never going to amount to anything."
    - "You can't do that."
    - "You won't be successful."
    - "Who do you think you are for doing that or charging that?"

- "Why would someone want to pay you for that?"
- "You're fat, ugly, no good, boring (insert derogatory comment here)."

- Someone you love or respect:
  - Hits or abuses you physically.
  - Emotionally abuses you with his or her words, such as with the comments above.
  - Hurts you or others you love in any way.
  - Completely doesn't support your goals or dreams.
  - Doesn't allow you to do what you want, making you feel trapped.

- It also could apply if the person in question says any of the following:
  - "Oh, don't do that. It will cost too much."
  - "Oh, don't do that. You could get hurt."
  - "Oh, don't do that. You could fail and lose money."
  - "Why don't you just stay home and be a mom?"
  - "Don't worry about all that business stuff. You don't need that."
  - "Why do you want to start your own business anyway?"

By the way, if you are in any of the harmful situations above, please get help from a professional. Call 911 if you are in physical danger. Don't just read this and do nothing, because that is NOT a normal situation.

Obviously, there are some of you who tend to make rash decisions often. For you, it might be helpful to have someone in your life to run things by first so you're not wasting time and money in the wrong places. Not everyone out there is as rational as I am. That's my little disclaimer for this section.

Working with partners

What I want to say about this topic is that, for the most part, you want to treat your partner as if he were your significant other. By partner, I'm referring to a business partner. That person could be your significant other, your long-time friend, acquaintance, or investor.

Do some relationship counseling before you enter into a business situation if you'll be working closely together in the running of the business to make sure you are thinking similarly in regards to the direction and management of the business.

Definitely get legal advice, and draw up legal agreements for all parties and possibilities that could occur to cover your bases.

I've seen way too many partnerships go sour. In fact, I can only think of four married couples of my friends and clients who run their businesses smoothly and successfully without killing each other. And I don't have any current examples to share of successful partnerships with non-married individuals.

I know dozens of examples, however, of marriages breaking up and friendships being destroyed by a horribly run or not well thought out partnership.

Some of the biggest issues seem to be:

- ❧ Not communicating the big picture goals for each person up front.
- ❧ Goals and visions changing and not fitting the partnership anymore.
- ❧ Someone deciding to go it alone and asking to buy the other out.
- ❧ Conflicts arising that can't be resolved.
- ❧ Not having the correct legal entities and documents in place from day one.

I don't typically recommend partnerships at all in business.

Typically, the main reason I see some partnerships start to develop is because individually the partners don't believe in themselves enough to go it alone. They think that by partnering up with someone else, it will be easier for them, easier to get clients, more supportive. Instead it's just a crutch to get them past their own confidence struggle.

Having mentors

This is one of the best things you can do for yourself and your business. Whether you want to uncover some of your limiting beliefs with a life coach, mindset mentor, or intuitive, or you want to design a kick-butt business and marketing plan with a business coach, finding the right mentor is the key to getting further faster.

I recommend you do whatever it takes to surround yourself with people and mentors who support and inspire you all the time. I will never be without at least one mentor in my life, now that I know what's possible when I have one.

What do you want to look for in a mentor?

It could be different for everyone, but typically what I look for in mentors are the following five things:

1. Do they have a specific and proven communication strategy, meaning they have a system you can follow to get the results you want? Do they actively interact and communicate with you about your options?

2. Do you trust them? This one is simple; it's either a gut yes or no. If no, then hold off hiring them and keep searching.

3. Do they have what you want in a specific area, meaning are they running their business like you want to run yours for the most part? (No one will be an exact fit, but it's easier to learn from someone who's doing what you want to do.)

4. Do they inspire you? This is a big one. They need to make you feel good about yourself, motivate you to take action, and encourage you to go after your dreams and more.

5. Are they still relevant, meaning they are still doing what they're teaching, or are they just preaching it now and not really in the trenches anymore?

It's very important to choose a mentor who walks her talk and who's still in the trenches doing what she teaches, in my opinion.

Those gurus out there teaching stuff they created years ago, but not still actively doing it, could have old and outdated information.

You want someone who's up on the latest in technology, industry, and marketing trends and someone who continues her own learning and mentoring as well.

Even if that mentor is just a few steps ahead of you, learning what she knows now that you don't know can shave off years of time and tens of thousands of dollars of investment.

If I only knew then (when I first started my business) what I know now, boy, I'd be a millionaire by now. But it's not about fast tracking to a million the first year; hardly anyone I know does that.

You want to be realistic when you set your goals, while still thinking really big.

Other factors to consider when hiring mentors:

- They have similar values to yours.
- They have confidence in what they do.
- They love what they do.
- They are happy.
- They are making money (if they're teaching you how to make more money).
- They can see your big vision and even think bigger for you.
- They are positive influences.
- They are well-connected.
- They genuinely care about your success.
- They focus on getting you results.
- You have adequate access to them when you need them. (Some gurus charge a lot of money

to work with them but then hardly offer any personal time with them.)

Oftentimes, your mentor will be your competition, like a few of my clients have been. I work with many business and marketing coaches around the world. It's fine with me. There's plenty of business for all of us. I'm happy to share with them what I know about building and growing a successful multiple six-figure business. They need to know this stuff because they're working too hard!

And although some similar clients know what to do as far as building and marketing their business, they sometimes end up coming to me for entirely different reasons, such as accountability, team-building, self-worth and confidence-building, learning how to sell, leveraging, and monetizing their efforts more.

Are you ready for a mentor now? Which kind?

Sometimes you can have more than one at a time depending on the specialties and how much you can handle.

Where do you look?

I say ask for referrals or go to the live events of the people you're considering. It's always best to hire them in person or from a referral. Plus, you often get the best deals in person.

Giving and receiving

How do you show people love daily? Do you think about how to exude love daily or what that would mean for others to experience?

Do you treat others like you want to be treated, or do you judge them, criticize them, and talk down to them every so often? (Sometimes even without knowing you're doing it?)

What you do on a day-to-day basis in everyday life also affects your love-filled environment.

If you cuss at the car that cuts you off or flip the finger at the person ahead of you driving too slowly, what are you telling the Universe?

You're saying, "I only want to show love when I feel like it."

How do you think that affects your karma or law of attraction ratings?

I believe it's important to try to exude love and caring all day, every day. I do it on my coaching calls, in emails I send, with door-to-door salespeople or store clerks. It's part of my daily life.

Don't get me wrong; every once in a while I slip up. I'm not perfect. However, I'm always aware of when I slip up, and I immediately make up for whatever it was I just let slip.

This goes for giving to charitable causes, too. Do you have a standard group that you regularly give to or charity rules you follow?

I'm just now sorting some new rules out for me, actually, as the more I make, the more I do want to give.

I typically support women business organizations since women entrepreneurs are my ideal clients. I support most animal shelters and causes because I love animals, especially dogs. I also donate to cancer organizations since a few people close to me have battled cancer and won.

I also do a few random and outrageous things occasionally that blow me and everyone I know away. The biggest of these being the time I donated $50,000 to the eWomenNetwork Foundation in a live auction at one of their annual conferences.

It's quite a funny story, actually. I'll share it with you later on in the book when it may make more sense however.

eWomenNetwork is my favorite women's business organization, and it happens to be one of the largest, too. Their foundation primarily helps women and children or young adults in the US or outside who want to better themselves. They do so much good with the funds they raise that I had no problem being such a big contributor to that organization. You'll want to check it out for networking, too, if you haven't heard of it.

Since that event, there have been other inspiring shows geared towards generous giving on television, such as *The Secret Millionaire*. One of my mentors, Ali Brown, was featured and now continues to support the charities she encountered on the show.

The main reason I talk so much about money throughout this book is because if we make more money, we can give more.

Where or what would you contribute to if you were inspired to donate $50,000 or more? Think about it, and we'll come back to this, but this kind of giving and receiving does affect your success. The year I donated that money to the foundation is the first year I hit six-figures in my business.

Loving life

Are you finally ready to love yourself fully, live a bigger life, and become the success you know you're meant to be?

If you're here already, then great. If not, what do you need to do to love your life more?

Are there too many naysayers or toxic people in your life?

Do you have too much head trash going on?

Do you need more love and passion in your love relationship?

If so, it's time to make some changes.

ACTION STEP

Decide what needs to change in your life, your business, or with whom you're surrounding yourself. How can you clear the negative, toxic energy in your life to open yourself up for more positive energy that feeds you?

Uncover what truly motivates you to be your greatest self and make sure you take steps to be in that energy on a daily basis. Energy and your environment play a really big part in the overall success of your business, so start realizing what needs to change.

There is a great recording on my regular website entitled The 3 Keys to Transforming Your Business to Fit Your Lifestyle. It helps you think bigger about your life, your vision, and your mindset, and it's free. You can get access to it and a few other free gifts when you visit **www.JumpstartYourMarketing.com/gifts**.

"You are the average of the five people you spend the most time with."

❀ Jim Rohn

Chapter 7

Step Seven—
Love For What You're
Doing

Loving your business

What are you doing now for your career or profession? Is it what you are truly meant to be doing for the rest of your life?

If you're in a J-O-B while you're reading this, then probably not.

If you already have your own business, then it's either a resounding "YES!" or an "I'm not sure," which really means, "No, probably not."

The goal of this chapter is to help you decide whether you're doing what you should be doing. Once you are absolutely sure, or at least you make the decision to find out what else is possible for you, then we can help you figure out what that looks like and how to make a bunch of money doing it.

So if you think you're good now, then answer the following questions first, and if your answer to all of them is a "Yes," then great; regardless, keep reading.

❧ Are you truly passionate about what you're doing?

- Does what you do make you want to jump out of bed in the morning and get to it?
- Do you love what you're doing so much that you would do it for free?
- Does what you offer make a big impact on your customers or clients?
- Are you constantly investing in yourself to learn more, be more, and find ways to make more?
- Do you truly believe in yourself that what you offer, your expertise, and what you charge is totally worth it?

Now, for those of you who are doing something you don't love, I would imagine you didn't give so many yeses.

That's OK, but what isn't OK is staying where you are and settling for what you're doing now. Why would you do that?

For security? Money? Benefits? Stability? Kids?

If you're doing something for those reasons, you are undervaluing yourself and settling, plain and simple. There are so many ways to make money these days, online and offline; it amazes me why some people would prefer to be miserable or even remotely unhappy.

I'm not a family therapist, but I'm just guessing that being miserable or unhappy doesn't help your family; it hurts it. Being miserable or unhappy makes you sick more often, too. Who wants to be sick? Being sick more often due to being miserable, depressed, or unhappy could lead to worse diseases. There are many examples of that.

Happiness and joy help to fight disease and stress. In fact, I have one friend who beat cancer thanks in large part to her happy, focused mental attitude, all without any harsh drugs, too.

So I'm not telling you you'll be healthier if you do what you love, but, come on, it is bound to make a huge impact on your overall health and well-being.

It's up to you.

What's your purpose?

Your purpose, however, is not about exactly what you're doing. It's more about the big picture of what you're doing.

I've only done a little training about purpose, but it's more than you may have done, so let me share what I've learned.

I've heard Tim Kelley speak about his theories and his book, *True Purpose*; I highly recommend this book.

He talks about your true purpose as the difference you are meant to make that is authentically yours.

In his book, Tim says, "Your purpose isn't a single vague, 'purpose statement'; it is a precise and detailed map for living a deeply fulfilling, powerful, and passionate life."

One of the exercises in his book involves having conversations with God, writing down questions in a journal that you want to know the answers to, then listening for the answers within yourself and writing down what comes to you. It's a pretty fascinating concept. At first I was pretty skeptical. I thought, "How do I know this isn't just my words coming out?"

But I've used this practice now when I really need some big guidance. For example, what sort of content should I deliver at my live event? What is the information and inspiration that my attendees really need to hear now? When I did that ten months before my first big event, I sat still and waited, then pages of pages of content came through me onto the paper. It was amazing.

Another thing Tim talks about in his book is your blessing. You can look at your purpose in regards to what your blessing is instead of making a purpose statement. Here's the difference:

Purpose statement based on essence: "I am a beacon of joy."

Purpose statement based on blessing: "My blessing is to create abundance and new possibilities."

Purpose statement based on mission: "My mission is to engage the nation in possibility."

I'm sure you're curious as to what my purpose is. My blessing is this:

> My blessing is to inspire all women to love themselves fully, live big, and leverage themselves to complete happiness.

There's a lot more to it than just deciding what you think it is yourself. I encourage you to go find out, one way or another, what your true purpose is, either with Tim's book or other means.

I mentioned earlier that I've had my palms read. Another way to find out what your purpose is is to have that done. You would look for a hand analyst. I've listed a couple for you plus many other recommendations on the book resources page at **www.LoveYourselfSuccessful. com/bookresources**.

What do you need to step into?

If you know your purpose, like I know mine, it could be quite expansive. You may have no earthly idea of how you will be able to fulfill it. This is pretty common.

I was at an event once with over 300 entrepreneurs in the room. In fact, it was an event featuring my friend who does hand analysis. She had analyzed everyone's hands prior to the event, and, boy, there was quite a stir in the crowd, in a good way.

Many of them had been told their purpose was enormously big in comparison to what they really thought they were capable of doing. Some of them were told they were meant to change the world in one way or another.

Others had been told they were supposed to be "in the spotlight" doing their purpose. In the spotlight could mean many things, but for this crowd mostly it meant speaking on stage, being very visible in their community, industry, or online. The introverts in the room who were given this purpose were freaking out.

I, of course, desire to be in the spotlight, I thrive on it. At that event, she told me my purpose was to be a big shot healer in the spotlight.

"Healer?" I said. In my head, I thought, "But I'm a business and marketing coach; I'm a mentor, not a healer."

Come to find out, which is also why I was meant to write this book, is that I am here to heal women on a grand scale.

I am here to help people start, grow, and market their businesses, but just like my Blessing, this purpose reading targeted how I would help women change the way they're feeling about themselves, how to love themselves fully, and how to stretch themselves into the success they're meant to be.

Hence, this book was birthed.

Do you think your purpose is much bigger than you're capable of achieving?

What do you have to be or become in order to step into your purpose?

Of course, you can deny your true calling and revert back to what's comfortable...but that's no fun. So let's go!

Overcoming fears of success

Imagine having a fear of success. I know people do, but I just can't imagine it. I've always wanted success. Although, I also wanted recognition and attention when I was young. I was an only child for the first ten years of my life. That may have something to do with it.

Believe it or not, a lot of women have fears of becoming successful or getting too big.

Sometimes it's based on the fact we don't like what we see out in the world today or the news; other successful people aren't always doing the right things or making the right decisions. Not to mention the paparazzi!

Also, if we get too big and successful, then that means:

- 💗 We won't have fun anymore.
- 💗 We'll be working too hard and long.
- 💗 We may not see our families as much.
- 💗 We'll have more responsibility.
- 💗 We'll have more stress.

❦   We'll have to be more accountable.

It doesn't have to be all that bad, however. That's why you build a team! I've got over five assistants in any given month who work for me doing various business- and marketing-related tasks. This is how I get so much done.

Delegating gets addictive, in case you're one of those control freaks out there saying, "Oh, no way will I delegate anything. No one can do it like I can." Trust me, it is awesome.

I can't tell you that getting bigger and more successful means less work. In the beginning it could mean more work, but if you design your business the right way from the start, you will have less stress and trouble doing this.

Imagine the rewards, though. What if you become so successful you can serve hundreds, thousands, or millions of people with whatever you end up doing?

Think of the global impact you can make for future generations. Look at women who are doing this, like Oprah Winfrey. Oprah started from nothing. You can do this too.

Expressing your authentic self

Business, these days, is personal. If you think you're going to get away with not sharing about your life or not posting pictures and videos about yourself, you're sorely mistaken. As a solopreneur (small business owner, entrepreneur), you _are_ your business.

This is a good thing, though. The more you share, the more your prospects will like, trust, and connect with you. Keep in mind that not everyone will like what you have to say, but 100% of the right people will!

Everything you do can become public knowledge, especially with social media.

Of course, you can always take precautions when it comes to your kids or family in general. That's not what I'm talking about.

I'm talking about what I'm doing here in this book. I'm sharing my story and experiences with you. I'm sharing the lessons I've learned and giving you tips, advice, and resources on how to make your life better based on what I've learned.

In case you can't tell, I'm being completely transparent and authentic with you about everything. I do this because:

1. I have nothing to hide.
2. I want you to learn from my mistakes.
3. I want you to be successful and happy.

Plain and simple: You should want to do the same with whatever you do in your business. If you do, it will show, and more people will follow you, recommend you, refer you, forward your information, and also buy from you.

Redefining your goals and dreams

As we go through this book, you'll probably want to continue revisiting the initial goals and ultimate lifestyle you outlined, as your goals and vision may continually get bigger. At least, I hope they will!

What do you believe you can do or have now that you didn't necessarily believe when you first picked up this book?

🌱 Make more money?

- 💗 Help more people?
- 💗 Not work so hard?
- 💗 Do something you're truly passionate about and make money at it?
- 💗 Be fully loved and supported?

I hope many of these and more.

In the next few chapters, we're going to move into the matter of money and what else is possible regarding making more money.

It's important to look at both your mindset around love and money in order to be completely successful, because with just money you're not probably going to be happy and with just love you could be pretty poor.

So let's help you figure out how to get both, shall we?

ACTION STEP

Do you know your true purpose? If not, go check out Tim Kelley's book on the book resources page I developed for you at **www.LoveYourselfSuccessful. com/bookresources**. Think about how long you are going to stay in a job or business that doesn't make you completely happy if that's your current situation. Give yourself a deadline to get out of it. Develop the action plan to make that happen.

Now think about what types of fears you may be facing. List them out or journal about them and where you think they stem from. Becoming aware of your fears and blocks is the first step to getting over them.

"Life is a journey from one point to another. You know where you will end up, but you don't know what route will get you there."

❧ Jennifer Robinson

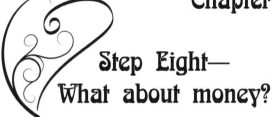

Chapter 8

Step Eight—
What about money?

Can money make you happy?

Let's first address why I talk about having a six- or seven-figure business so much in this book and in my coaching.

For the majority of entrepreneurs I know and have run across, I believe:

- ❧ The more you make, the more you will give, therefore changing the world.

- ❧ The more you make, the more empowered you become to make even more changes.

- ❧ The more changes you make, the more impact you create, hopefully reaching hundreds of thousands of people.

- ❧ We are all responsible for creating more awareness, goodness, and love.

For me, money makes me happy because:

- ❧ I don't have to worry about bills being paid or a roof over my head, then I can just serve and give freely and abundantly of my advice and inspiration.

- ❦ It allows me to travel the world and inspire thousands of other women entrepreneurs to love themselves successful.

- ❦ It allows me the simple pleasures I enjoy, like fine wine, entertaining friends, fun clothes, and accessories

- ❦ It allows me to give generously whenever I see the need; giving $20 to a homeless person, buying someone a coffee, donating $1,000 to a non-profit, doing good in the community, and celebrating with loved ones.

- ❦ It provides me necessities to keep me and my dog, Zeke, healthy.

When I talk to some women about making really large sums of money, they just don't get it. They only want to make just what they need to get by because they don't want to take more than their share.

These women will eat Top Ramen noodles before they ask for more money. I don't think that's any way to serve others. If you have a really important purpose or message to deliver or service to provide, you should definitely take good care of yourself first so that you can serve more people on an even deeper level.

Lisa Nichols from the book *The Secret* once said in a talk, "You've got to serve from your saucer and not your cup." That means that what's in the cup is for you, and what's left in the saucer is the energy you have left over to give to others. Too many women serve from their cup, the energy they need to thrive, then they're always in need, sick, or down on their luck.

If you do that, stop it. It's more than OK to make a lot more money; you ARE worth it.

What is the bigger WHY that you're on this planet for? What is the real reason you're doing what you're doing?

My bigger why is to inspire 100,000 women entrepreneurs or more to create at least six-figure businesses.

Whatever your bigger WHY is, it needs to be your motivation to want to make more money—lots of money!

What will you do with more money?

I have one client who has a non-profit rescue for dogs and wants to go global.

I know another gentleman who goes to Africa and builds schools, helping the women there get an education.

I personally would love to travel and speak more in person, while also providing more resources virtually to millions of women all over the world. I want to teach and empower these women who are starting up their own businesses and who don't want to waste money in the wrong places. I want to show them what to do, how to do it, and how to start making money fast.

However, to do that effectively and practically, I need funding for my trips, travel, workshop planning, marketing, and much more.

Of course, I would donate more, too; I will choose some additional causes and organizations very soon, I'm sure. But first I still need to leverage more of the money I am making into other investments to build more long-term wealth. That's the big picture plan, at least, to diversify my portfolio.

It's a very important step that many Internet market-ers and online business owners aren't doing these days. They're buying the big houses, fancy private jets, and what happens when the Internet isn't as reliable as it is today? You just never know.

OK, so of course I do want a little newer house, but not much bigger. (Unless there's a man in it with me!) My current house will be a rental. I have a car that I like, and it's paid off; I'm not too big on flashy cars, so that's not a really big deal.

I do want to take a few more vacations a year. But who doesn't? I haven't seen the world yet; I've been too busy building up this business.

I can see the horizon, however, and it doesn't have to take you as long as it has taken me. If you start now, and get direction from the right people to help you, you can move a lot faster than I did to get to the income I am at now.

Have I given you ideas for what YOU want to do with the big money you're going to make?

If so, what are they, and what is your bigger WHY?

Allowing yourself to receive

Some of you may not need to read this part, but more of you probably do need to read it.

Allowing yourself to receive comes from knowing you deserve it, then accepting the income, the rewards, the compliments, the bonuses, and more.

I know a lot of women who don't allow themselves to receive very often. Here are a few things you could possibly be doing. Check yourself:

- ❧ You work overtime with a client but don't charge them for the extra time.

- ❧ When someone tries to pay you or give you a tip or extra money, perhaps you reject it, saying something like, "That's not necessary."

- ❧ If someone compliments you, instead of simply saying, "Thank you," you downplay it with a negative remark about yourself or whatever it was they mentioned.

You want to get in the habit of accepting and receiving; this is the only way that more money is going to come to you. You know that, right?

You have to let in the money, gifts, or messages that are coming to you now, or more may not come.

How can you do that?

You want to practice receiving everything that comes your way:

- ❧ Say "thank you" to all compliments you receive, then be quiet.

- ❧ For prospects who want to buy from you, ask for their money on the spot. Don't wait until they have to practically twist your arm to take it.

- ❧ Prize drawings: It's funny. Sometimes I'll be at an event where there is a raffle drawing, and one woman will buy a bunch of tickets and win three or more of the prizes but will want to give some of them back thinking she doesn't deserve to have that many, when, in fact, she did deserve it. She bought a bunch of tickets and had a better chance; that's why she won so many. Accept multiple prizes or other good things that come your way.

- ❧ Someone may allow you to cut in front of them in line at the grocery store because you just have a couple items and they have a full cart. Instead of accepting their invitation to step in front of them, you say "No, that's OK." Why do you do that? Accept their kindness.

- ❧ Someone may want to buy you a drink when you're out, or your friend offers to pay for lunch when you get together. Why do we always fight over who pays the tab? Let others pay if they offer.

What similar scenarios can you think of from your day-to-day life? How can you accept more that comes your way?

Believing in abundance

What are your beliefs around money?

Remember before when I wrote that without the right mindset around love and money, it doesn't matter what amount of marketing you do or what systems you put in place, it will be difficult to really make any big money?

If you're afraid to charge what you're worth, or afraid to invest in yourself or your business accordingly, it could be that you don't believe in abundance.

Money is energy. It is the flow of money everywhere around you constantly that creates abundance. Yet many people are scared to spend or invest their money, which means they're halting the flow.

I was in a workshop recently about money, sales, and making more money. There were about seventy people in the room for three days. The workshop was designed to teach us how to sell our wares so that by the end of the three days we would all make money from one another in the room.

What happened amazed me. In just three short days, the seventy of us sold to each other over $30,000 worth of our products and services. We didn't sell to outside sources, only people in the room. It was basically a micro-economy that we formed.

Why it was amazing is that everyone made money. The people who were afraid to sell made money. The people who didn't know how to ask for the sale made money. Even the people who didn't start out with anything to sell figured something out and made money.

But no one withheld their money. They bought products and services, even though they maybe couldn't afford too much. They bought just what they needed, and it all came back to them in the long run because others bought their products and services, too.

This is what is supposed to happen in your world, too. Are you doing things to halt the flow of money coming back to you?

If you think of money as just being energy that needs to flow, maybe you can understand more about how you can make more money.

I believe there is an abundance of money out there because I've seen it. I've seen friends of mine make millions of dollars at one three-day event, for example. I've seen friends of mine go from a couple hundred thousand dollars one year to multiple millions the next.

I've experienced exponential growth in my own business, too. It really does seem that the more I invest in my business or myself, the more I end up making in revenue that year. I've always experienced growth every year that I've been in business. I have never gone backwards, not even in the economic slumps we've had.

As I said before, I really attribute most of that to having complete faith—investing in myself so the money continues to flow but also taking inspired action towards my goals.

If you're feeling stuck around money, think about how you're holding on to it or viewing it. Ask yourself if you truly believe you will be successful and that there is an abundance of money.

If you don't believe in yourself, or have faith your business will work out and make you big money, then it probably won't. And if you don't invest properly and continuously in yourself and your business, then you're probably still too comfortable in your life or your business. For some reason, you aren't willing to step outside your comfort zone and truly go for all it is that you want.

What are you worth?

I'm on a secret quest to get everyone who charges by the hour to also find ways to sell packages of time with bonuses that add value. Then you can charge more, work less, and sell less often.

I'm also on a quest to get everyone to think of herself as worth a minimum of $200 per hour. I know that's a stretch for some of you who've never even made over $20 or $50 per hour. But trust me, there are ways you can serve, teach, and sell to position yourself that way. You just aren't yet aware of how to do this.

For example, I have a client I will call "Suzy." Suzy has a training company where she does presentations for larger corporations and organizations. Suzy custom creates and sells each presentation she does, creating multiple hours of preparation time before as well as following her presentation. Yet, Suzy doesn't count all the hours she spends in setup or follow-up when she quotes the price of the presentation.

Suzy thinks she's making $200 per hour since she's billing out $1,600 for an eight-hour day. Yet, when we crunched the numbers on how much time and effort Suzy really spends on each presentation or customer, it was more like eighteen hours total. Therefore, Suzy really makes $89 per hour per presentation, less than half of what she feels she is worth.

Suzy was undervaluing herself because she hadn't properly structured the business model or her pricing in a way to reflect her true worth. In fact, Suzy should be charging the client $3,600 for a full day custom presentation.

See what happens? Are you doing anything remotely similar to this scenario? Think about it.

If you're saying to yourself, "I'm worth way more than $200 per hour," then fabulous!

But if you're not, and you have no idea what would make you worth so much money, then we need to work on that. Every client or prospect I've ever met is worth at least that. I'm sure you have so much knowledge and expertise in whatever it is that you do that you should charge at least $200 an hour for it. If you really don't think your abilities warrant that high a fee, then you could be doing the wrong thing! You need to realize this, and fast, so you can start charging what you're truly worth, and getting it!

Business Math 101

Do you know how easy it can be to make $1,000,000 per year? Let's crunch some numbers here, so I can show you.

Here's a little table I like to use at workshops to show just how easy it can be. You just need to have the right price for your programs, products or services.

Business Math 101:

$1 x 1,000,000 = $1,000,000

$10 x 100,000 = $1,000,000

$100 x 10,000 = $1,000,000

$1,000 x 1,000 = $1,000,000

$10,000 x 100 = $1,000,000

$100,000 x 10 = $1,000,000

$1,000,000 x 1 = $1,000,000

There are people out there who think they're going to get rich selling $20 or $40 products like juices, supplements, jewelry, artwork, trinkets, or whatever it may be. But, look at that chart.

How many $10 things do you have to sell in a year to make $1,000,000? You have to sell 100,000 things. That's a heck of a lot, I say.

How many people do you have to talk to in order to sell to that many people? Probably double that number, at least, because you won't sell to everyone you meet. And that is only if you are very proactive and successful with a 50% close ratio.

How many people do you have to talk to every day in order to talk to 200,000 people in a year? Count only how many weekdays are in a year. You have to talk with 770 **NEW** prospects EVERY DAY! Wow, that's just crazy to me, and not really realistic, if you think about it, right?

That count is with no vacation days, days off, or sick days; think of what you'd have to make up if you took a day off!

OK, so it's not as bad when you're selling something for $100, or maybe $1,000, but most entrepreneurs aren't even selling stuff for $1,000.

Think of how much easier it is if you have a program or service for $10,000; then you only have to sell 100 of them every year to have a million dollar business. That sounds more like it to me!

Later on, I'll talk about how to create higher-priced programs, products, and services. If you can't imagine this for yourself just yet, you just don't know what you don't know. Be open to what's possible and what could be; you'll be amazed.

ACTION STEP

How do you feel about money? Do you believe there is an abundance available to you? Write down your thoughts and feelings around money—spending it, investing it, asking for it. Then write out what you would do with lots more of it? LOTS MORE!

What is your bigger WHY? Is there a bigger cause or movement you want to embrace, create, or contribute to?

Then do the math—the Business 101 Math I expressed just now. Is what you're selling practical to be able to get you to your overall money goals? Do you need to charge more, raise your rates, or figure out something else to sell to make the kind of money you really want to make? It could be that all you need is a little more confidence to be able to charge more for your products or services. It could be that you need one or two more business models with higher price points to add to your business.

I'd love to help you any way I can to figure out what you need to do to achieve your goals. One of your free gifts when you went to go grab that free audio recording on my main website was a complimentary business strategy session with me. If you haven't already gone and applied to do that, then now would be a good time to do that so we can figure out and plot out how you can make more money in your business doing what you love. Go to **www.AskKat.biz** for the details on how to access that free call with me now.

Chapter 9

Step Nine— Love and Money: How to Finally Have it All!

What comes first?

I believe you need to work on both love and money at the same time; they go hand-in-hand.

Unfortunately, for some of you, that could mean a lot of work if you're lacking in some way in the love department and also in money.

However, focusing on both allows more balance in your life, which is good.

You want to be focusing on your personal needs while you're building your successful business.

That definitely means careful scheduling of your to do's, tasks, and self-care time to start with.

Actually one of the first things I work on with my coaching clients is creating space for them.

We need to look at where and how you're spending your time every week so we can determine how to shift things around, disregard things, or even delegate them.

I have one client who I worked with who had two fulltime businesses, both grossing over $100,000 each year.

She had three kids and a husband, plus her marriage was suffering. You can imagine this was a busy gal.

With all the time-saving techniques, additional marketing strategies, and automated systems we put in place in her business and her life, we ended up saving eight hours a week of her time! That was huge for her.

Now her marriage is on the mend, and she has more time to devote to her growing kids' needs. She's also started another business that's even more leveraged.

So the key to having it all—more love, money, and freedom in your life—is to leverage.

- ♥ Leverage is about doing something once, then getting paid over and over again for it.

- ♥ Leverage is teaching or mentoring to many people at a time, rather than always one-on-one.

- ♥ Leverage is about creating higher ticket offerings to maximize your time and income.

- ♥ Leverage is about saving time doing something you were doing before yet finding a way to do it differently or more efficiently.

- ♥ Leverage is about outsourcing the tasks you don't like to do, don't know how to do, or don't want to do.

Here is a quick diagram of how I see leverage playing a part in building a happier, more successful life for you.

How does your world need to change based on these aspects?

Designing your life for an abundance of both

One of the reasons I wanted to write this book, *Love Yourself Successful*, is because I have seen so many entrepreneurs in my circle become successful. I know firsthand that it's possible, no matter what you do, what your business is, or in what industry you work.

Yet so many women entrepreneurs especially doubt themselves, or they don't see how they can have it all, the love, money, success, and happiness.

I wanted to share everything I know and have learned in order to motivate you, inspire you, and encourage you to live a bigger life, go for what you want, stop settling, and KNOW that you do deserve this all and you CAN have it.

You just may not know how to get there on your own, that's all, and that's OK. There's nothing wrong with asking for help.

You may find bits and pieces of how to become more successful in each book you read, or on websites, tele-classes, and eBooks.

But until you decide to get serious about building a successful six-plus-figure business so you can help more people with your gift, you probably won't reach that level of success, I'm afraid. Something will hold you back or keep you comfortable.

I wanted to bring the thoughts I had, but also the ones I've adopted from the million-dollar mentors I've worked with closely over the last few years, so that you could see what it takes to become that successful woman entrepreneur you know you're meant to be.

What I've found from extensive encounters and observation is that entrepreneurs who are making high six- or seven-figure incomes in their businesses have three very important behaviors in common. These three actions form the acronym BIG that I use for one of my own programs, The Live BIG Mastermind.

Living BIG means to:

1. BELIEVE: They have complete faith and belief in themselves and their abilities. They believe that no matter what, they will be successful, make money, do well, serve who it is they need to serve, and do so in a big way. They have NO PLAN B.

2. INVEST: They are continuously investing in themselves, their businesses, their team, their home life, and other opportunities that come up that make sense. They are always on the lookout for good moneymaking opportunities and are never too busy to notice them.

3. GIVE: They give on every level. That is one of their main priorities in life. Giving to others monetarily, giving to themselves the gift of self-care, giving freely of their advice, and so much more.

But there is one other attribute that these high achievers also have in common and that is:

4. ACTION: They constantly take inspired (imperfect) action towards what it is that they want, not letting anything get in their way—not their mindset, limiting beliefs, checkbook balance, friends or family, economic circumstances, mother nature, or anything else. If they get thrown a curveball (which all of us have), they get up, dust themselves off, and charge ahead again without fail.

How do you plan on living bigger in your life?

ACTION STEP

Deciding which to focus on first, love or money, could be a tough question for some of you because you're lacking in both departments right now. If that's the case, I recommend you start with the one that will increase your happiness and positive energy most first. That way you'll be in a better position and be more motivated to do what's needed to enhance both areas faster. Reflect back on the book and what you've discovered about yourself thus far and see where you're at.

"Take the first step in faith. You don't have to see the whole staircase. Just take the first step."

❧ Martin Luther King Jr.

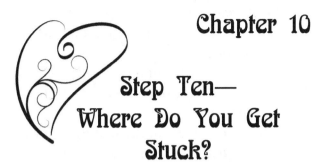

Chapter 10

Step Ten—
Where Do You Get
Stuck?

Why are you stuck?

What's keeping you from enjoying the successful life and business that you know you deserve and are meant to have?

Whether you can admit it now or know if this is true for you or not, it's usually one or more of the following feelings or thoughts:

- 💗 Fear
- 💗 Doubt
- 💗 Worry
- 💗 Security
- 💗 Subconscious belief
- 💗 Self-esteem
- 💗 Love

The year I went through that big emotional, internal mentoring and shift in my life was the year I learned all about the internal blocks that hold us back from getting what we want.

One of my mentors I mention in the book resources page online took me on this journey that, to me, was both fascinating and scary.

Many of the ideas in this chapter have come from this mentor and also from the book *Think and Grow Rich* by Napoleon Hill.

It has since come in quite handy in my coaching, since almost every one of my clients has had some sort of stuck pattern that we need to address.

Now is when we want to look at what could be holding you back.

Typically, most entrepreneurs don't achieve a six-plus-figure business for multiple reasons, such as:

- You don't believe in yourself 100%.
- You're not taking leaps of faith.
- You make decisions by your checkbook balance.
- You're undervaluing yourself.
- You don't know what you don't know.
- You're unwilling to learn.
- You think you KNOW what's best.
- You're not thinking BIG enough.
- You lack a support system.
- You're slow to make decisions.
- You miss or pass on opportunities.
- You're scared to be big or successful.
- You let the head trash control you.
- You self-sabotage and procrastinate.
- You're not clear enough on what's possible.

🌱 You don't focus enough on marketing.

🌱 You can't see HOW it will work out, and you need to know that before taking action.

🌱 You aren't implementing enough.

🌱 You have no systems; there's chaos behind the scenes.

🌱 You aren't delegating enough of the RIGHT tasks.

🌱 You're too busy to focus on SALES.

🌱 You may not BELIEVE you can really do it.

Do you relate to some of these, or do you have other concerns?

You want to get really serious with yourself here if things are going to change for you. Don't stay in denial or ignore these feelings and emotions; get them out and express them, then let's figure out a way for you to move on and thrive.

Limiting beliefs

Limiting beliefs are something most of us have to some extent about something.

Your thoughts, feelings, and actions create your beliefs, which in turn create your mind and how it reacts and makes decisions.

When we are babies and very young children, we are exposed to all kinds of opinions and expressions about love, self-worth, money, and more. Those opinions and expressions we are exposed to seep into our unconscious minds and create the beliefs we have today as adults.

This is why you make certain decisions and react in certain ways about all kinds of things, some in often very different ways than your significant other, friends, and family. We all have some thought or belief from our childhood that may not be the most positive or healthy for us.

The difference between successful people and not-so-successful people, however, is that successful people have figured out a way to get over their limiting beliefs or push through them and not let those beliefs control their destiny.

But before you can get over them, you have to understand what they are and why they are there in the first place.

For example, I've always had a need for love, recognition, and attention. That comes from being raised as an only child until I was about ten years old.

My parents were divorced, and my mom worked a lot, as far as I can remember. I recall playing board games by myself, being two or three different players in the game. It was a lonely experience, although I somehow made it fun.

I also remember waiting for my dad to come pick me up for a visit, and many times he was late—often days late. I felt a little unloved and like I wasn't as important to him as I wanted to be.

Those experiences somehow framed my thinking, so that I now like to be the life of the party. I enjoy being on stage talking to large groups. I like to make people laugh, getting the attention turned on me.

Also, in my personal love relationships, I prefer to have a lot of two-way attention, affection, and intimate communication.

Thankfully, these beliefs I formed weren't too harmful, if you think about all the bad things some people have gone through—maybe even you?

I've seen women come from hugely physically and mentally abusive families. Adults having gone through that type of situation (before seeking help) are often less trusting, don't feel safe and secure, are hesitant to commit in a personal love relationship, and are also somewhat defensive.

I've seen women come from families where there was hardly enough money to be able to feed the family and lack of money was a daily concern. Parents in that situation can either handle it in one of two ways: they can either live with a scarcity mindset and constantly worry that there may not be enough, or they can live with a positive mindset that "as long as we have each other and we're all healthy, we have exactly what we need." The two different ways of thinking and behaving by parents can create two entirely different kinds of belief systems for their children.

I'm not suggesting here that it's all our parents' fault, because they had parents too. It goes back generations. But if some of this insight speaks to you and what you could be engaging in with your family, kids, and loved ones, then you have the power to change yourself and the family mindset.

Many times we think we can easily rid ourselves of the limiting beliefs we have if, when we become aware of them, we make a decision to stop that behavior or thinking. But I've seen hundreds of women try this and the belief is still not gone; I don't think it's as easy as that.

The most common limiting beliefs that I see in the people I come in contact with in my business or out networking include the belief that:

- You have to work hard to make good money.
- You have to work longer hours to make big money.
- You can't afford it.
- You don't deserve it.
- You aren't worthy of it.
- You'll never be successful.
- Money doesn't make you happy.
- You don't know how, so why even try.
- You'll never be as rich or successful as them.
- You'll never make a lot of money.
- No one is perfect. You'll never find the perfect man with everything you want, so this one is good enough.

I'm writing this book because I don't want you to settle. I don't want you to settle for someone who is "good enough." I don't want you to settle for a job or business that's just "good enough" or "pays the bills." I don't want you to settle for a life without complete happiness, love, and all your true heart's desires.

I want so much more for you. Now it's time for you to want and claim that for yourself.

Self-sabotage

Self-sabotage is a very common problem I see with most women entrepreneurs I have known.

In one way or another, they are taking or not taking actions that sabotage their success or their path to success.

Self-sabotage goes back to the belief you have in yourself and the faith that you know if it will all work out.

We subconsciously, and sometimes consciously, sabotage ourselves so we don't have to:

- Become successful.
- Make more money.
- Work harder.
- Gain exposure.
- Be uncomfortable.

Some of these self-sabotaging habits look like:

- Procrastination.
- Disorganization.
- Busy work.
- Creating.
- Planning.
- Depression.
- Complaining.
- Settling.
- Doubting.
- Saying, "I can't afford that," instead of, "How can I afford that?"

Many times, when an opportunity comes into our lives that can help us become more successful or get us closer to our goals and dreams, we ignore it or don't even notice it.

We usually let it pass us by because we aren't sure how to incorporate it into our lives; we aren't sure how to do it or what will happen if we take advantage of it. That thinking will keep you limited.

What happens when an opportunity comes into your life?

Doubt comes in and takes a big bite out of your thoughts. The second you let doubt in, fear and worry follow behind.

When fear, doubt, and worry enter your life, your mind will fill in the rest, creating illusions that become your reality.

Illusions are things that we perceive as negative occurrences or roadblocks, but often, if we looked at them differently, they could be considered fantastic opportunities. Roadblocks are often just subconscious blocks that we put in front of ourselves so that we can sabotage our success and our lives. They come in the form of excuses.

The Universe will also bring roadblocks. Sometimes really tragic things can happen in your life to hold you back, such as deaths, loss of jobs or health, or worse. They can happen in multiples, too, if the Universe really wants to test you.

What matters is how you overcome those obstacles, breaking through, and continuing on the path to your goals. Don't let bad things that happen "be a sign" that you shouldn't continue; that's just an excuse you're using to sabotage yourself.

Caring what others think

To a certain extent, you want to be wary about caring what others think. Of course, as it relates to your overall values and safety, yes, you might consider others' thoughts and opinions.

But what I've found is that most people I know in my personal life, my long-time friends and family, really don't understand me and what I do.

Therefore, I have limited discussions with them around my goals, big visions, desires, and plans.

I can't afford to let any negative thoughts or actions into my life or my environment, and neither can you. Your energy is too precious, and you need all of it to continuously move forward on your journey.

Don't hang around people who don't think you're special, important, successful, or just totally awesome!

However, I have had mentors and model entrepreneurs in my life to whom I have compared myself. I would compare my level of success with what they've achieved or not achieved.

For a couple of years, my mental competition actually slowed my progress way down in my business; I was so worried all the time about, "Why are they buying from her and not me?"

What I learned over time, however, is that when you compare yourself to others, you never realize your own true greatness.

It's important that you believe you are great and worthy and trust that thousands of people can learn and be inspired from you in whatever you do.

You just need to know more than the people who you teach and inspire know. You don't have to be the biggest, most successful person in your industry in order to be completely successful.

If you own your power, people won't manipulate you, and you will attract 100% of the right clients.

Control-freak-itis

I had to throw this in here because, as a recovering control freak, I had to overcome a lot of things to get to the level of success I am at now. I'm sure that I will face even more to come on the journey ahead of me.

My wish for you, if there is a chance that you could be a control freak in any way, is that you find a way to let go so you can grow.

Letting go is one of the hardest things to do. I know. You can let go in many ways:

- ♥ Let go of doing it all yourself.
- ♥ Let go of your opinions on how something needs to be done.
- ♥ Let go of needing to be perfect.
- ♥ Let go of planning too much and not implementing.
- ♥ Let go of old ways of thinking how you'll become successful.

I can tell you that once you finally embrace the fact that you will need help, that is when you will start to see bigger success. Why not accept your need for help now?

I can tell you that you don't know what you don't know, and, therefore, you may not know the best way to take on a task or goal.

And I can tell you that once you stop planning for perfection and start just stepping out into uncharted waters, going after what you want, that is when you'll realize how easy it is.

More than likely, you're making it too difficult—life, your business, your kids' needs, your goals, your self-care. Stop working so hard at it all and recruit the help of systems, people, and models that are already out there to show you how to do it much more efficiently and effectively.

Getting unstuck

Getting unstuck from your limiting beliefs, negative circumstances, or people in your life could take an hour to do while reading this book, or it could take you a lifetime; it's hard to say. It depends on how bad you really want what you say you want and how much time and effort you devote to working on what's missing, what needs to be fixed, and how to achieve more success.

I'm confident you can achieve whatever you want, as long as you believe it also. It all stems back to your own self-confidence, though, and how much faith you have in yourself, your purpose, and why you're here, as well as how and who you're supposed to serve.

The power of belief:

If you can think it, you can do it. If your mind can produce an image of it, then it's got to be possible to achieve. Your thoughts create your outcome, so stop thinking negatively now.

Become aware of anything negative that slips out of your mouth, into your thoughts, and even in your actions.

Awareness is the first step.

This means that if you can see yourself making hundreds of thousands, or even millions, of dollars, but you have no idea how to get there, then that's OK. It is possible. You have to believe it and just start taking inspired action. Yes, you may take some wrong paths or actions, but the goal is to keep course-correcting along the way.

As long as you don't stop yourself thinking, "How long is it going to take me to get there, what am I doing wrong?" you'll get there.

Too many people stop themselves somewhere along the way. Either they lose momentum, lose confidence because they keep hearing no's, or they run out of money to invest in their journey.

Your job is not to know how you will do it before you begin your journey. Just know that you will succeed no matter what, then take the action that's right in front of your face today. Take the next action tomorrow, and the day after that, and the day after that. Never stop or give up.

Getting unstuck takes a clear decision and a lot of action. What you fail to change will be passed down to others, so why not create a more positive world for your children, loved ones, and yourself in the process?

ACTION STEP

What's keeping you from enjoying the successful life and business that you know you deserve and are meant to have?

Identify what limiting beliefs you think may be holding you back, if any. Think back to where those came from and really think if they're true or just illusions.

List out the ways you might be self-sabotaging yourself and your success.

Take note of where you may need to release some control in your life or your business. Where do you see that you're holding on too tight to something that can be delegated or released?

"Obstacles don't have to stop you. If you run into a wall, don't turn around and give up. Figure out how to climb it, go through it, or work around it."

~ Michael Jordan

Chapter 11

Step Eleven— What Needs to Change?

Preparing for change

The first thing you may want to do is clear space in your life in order to have time to change. Too many people make excuses for why they don't focus enough on themselves or their own self-development or self-care. Don't do that.

Instead, figure out where you're wasting time and energy, then repurpose that time and energy into more constructive activities that will allow you to change and/ or reach your goals faster.

One of the activities I like to have my coaching clients do, sometimes when we first begin, is to track their time.

Keep a journal, list, or spreadsheet of everything you spend time on every day for an entire week. Write down how much time you're spending checking emails, surfing the Internet, posting on Facebook, running errands, doing laundry, shuffling your kids around, cooking meals, shopping, and actually working and getting paid.

Then after a week, look back at that list and you should see a whole lot of areas where you aren't maximizing your time. If you don't see any, have someone else look at the list, because they're there.

There will be things you don't like to do, don't want to do, aren't good at doing, and then think of the things that aren't even on the list that should be. What are you neglecting in your personal life, your business, your marketing, and more?

The biggest step you can do now is to get some of those activities off your plate.

Find someone to do them for you, someone who is better at them than you or likes to do certain things that you maybe don't.

Figure out how to systematize or automate some of the things you're doing. There are usually easier, more efficient ways to do most things, but you may not necessarily think of them, so ask someone else if she has ideas.

Then determine what activities you just need to stop doing, at least for the short term.

If you really need to make some big changes in your life or your business to get what you want, then you may want to stop doing some of the things you're doing, such as:

- Volunteering. It's hard to truly help others when you are in need of help yourself first (think of the cup and saucer scenario).

- Housework and yard work. Someone else can do this, or just leave it for a short time and focus on you. No one will die if this stuff does not get done.

- Saying yes to everything. Are you constantly agreeing to be on committees, organization boards, or the mom who always runs the neighborhood kids around? You have a life, too, and you don't want to be the doormat others always rely on or take advantage of for their convenience. Start saying no.

- 🐝 Shopping for things you can do more efficiently online. I used to love to shop. I'd shop once a week, just to feel better—you know, retail therapy. This isn't an efficient use of your time, however; you most likely don't need something every week, do you?

- 🐝 Insert your biggest time sucker here.

Occasionally I order my groceries online to be delivered. Ask yourself, "Do I really need to pick out my own tomatoes?"

Just in the last couple months, I've ordered online a new BBQ, clothes, gift cards, and wine; I even send greeting cards online.

In fact, when I go to a department store, I usually plan ahead and book a personal shopper for myself so I can maximize my time. Personal shoppers are a free service, and it can save you a ton of time because you tell them what you're looking for and they go find it for you, speeding up your time in the store.

Now, some of you could be thinking, "But I like to shop, it's fun." I'm telling you that I thought that way for years too, but now, making multiple six figures and having bigger goals to achieve, more success, and fun in my business is much more fun to me than random shopping experiences. You have to trust me on this.

So, the first step in preparing for change is to make room to be able to change. Otherwise you will have an excuse that you don't have time to do what it takes…no excuses!

Sometimes you have to pay to play

No excuses means not holding yourself back financially, either. I realize, for some of you, this isn't as easy as it may seem.

You or your family may be experiencing a financial setback, such as a foreclosure, layoff, death, taxes, or unplanned emergency.

However, there's never going to be a good time to invest in yourself.

You'll never just have a bunch of money to hand off or invest in your own learning, self-development, business-development, etc.; it's just not in the budget. You have to put it in the budget, though.

There will never be a good time to take advantage of an opportunity or leap of faith. There could always be some circumstance or perceived obstacle standing right in the way.

It doesn't matter. If you let yourself succumb to this way of thinking and these circumstances, then guess what? You aren't going to be the success you're meant to be, are you? You'll be like 95% of the rest of the US making under $100,000 per year.

You can be more.

You can do more.

You can have more.

But sometimes you have to pay to play. To me, paying to play means that you need to sometimes invest financially in getting where you want to go.

So many entrepreneurs want to build their business on a shoestring and want to invest the least amount of money they can, yet they want to be millionaires. That thinking doesn't really compute.

Of course, there are some very inexpensive ways to build, grow, and market your business to start making money. It's very doubtful that you will get to be extremely successful, making over six figures or more, without investing some along the way. I'd say that you might have to invest at least 10-40% of what you want to make in order to get there. That means if you want to make $50,000 one year, you may want to plan to invest $5,000-$20,000 to be able to get there. That's a good investment isn't it?

What about if you want to reach $100,000? Then investing $40,000 isn't totally unrealistic.

I'm referring to investing in mentors, training programs, marketing plans, and training, but it might be a different kind of investing as well.

Let me share why this phrase: "Sometimes you've got to pay to play" has special meaning to me.

It happened a couple years ago, when I was attending a big, out-of-town women's business conference with over 2,500 other women.

Every year, this organization I belong to, eWomen-Network, holds their annual conference. On the first night, they used to hold a big live auction at dinner. The prizes normally included trips around the country to meet various big name people in business with the purpose of being connected to them and gaining resources or access to bigger opportunities in your industry or your business.

The year prior, I knew about this auction, but I didn't come prepared to bid on anything and had no idea the kind of money one would bid and invest in such opportunities. It was upwards of $10,000 for each experience.

So the next year, I came prepared, or so I thought. I came with the intention of investing up to $10,000 in one of these experiences if I thought it could help me grow my business in some way.

During the live auction, there was so much happening; the lights were low, the auctioneers spoke fast, and the bidding hands went up like crazy. This time some bids started at $10,000!

I began to get a little nervous. What if I don't win anything? I only came prepared to bid $10,000.

I watched and listened to the experiences being explained. No, I didn't care about Estee Lauder and the beauty industry. I didn't care about Hollywood and the movie industry.

Then it came to the last prize.

They splashed a picture of Oprah on the big screen above me, and my hand instantly went up in the air to make a bid. "$10,000," I said. I didn't even know what the whole experience entailed, but I knew in my gut that I had to do it.

Before I knew it, the bidding was going up in $5,000 dollar increments. It quickly rose to $30,000, then $40,000, then $50,000 and to $67,000…and I was still bidding!

At that moment, it was between me and one other woman way across the room. The CEO and founder of eWomenNetwork brought us up on stage to negotiate further, as they often do in these bidding wars.

We haggled for a bit and finally both of us agreed to pay $50,000 each to go on this trip. Everything was paid for pretty much, and we were to meet one of Oprah's radio show producers, see a taping of one of the shows, and basically that was it.

But being in marketing, I knew that I could spin this into all kinds of different opportunities. I just didn't know what they were right at that time. I bid in faith, I won in faith, and I invested to the non-profit foundation in faith that, because I gave in such a big way, I was bound to receive. I trusted in the Universe to bring me very good fortune and opportunities resulting from this big step.

People often ask me, "So, what did you get out of that experience, Katrina? Was it worth it?"

I had no idea what could have become of this opportunity had I stopped to think about it during the auction. I could have stopped myself from bidding, rationalizing, "Where will I get the money?" or, "What kind of return on investment (R.O.I.) is this going to bring?" but I didn't. I leapt in faith as I always do. I went with my gut, which was strongly pushing me to do this. I felt that if I ignored the feeling, it would be a huge missed opportunity.

Now, from a practical state in looking back on it all, here are some conclusions to the story and my R.O.I., in case you're wondering:

My first goal with bidding in the first place was my deep desire that year to get exposure at this event and get on stage so I was noticeable to not only the eWomenNetwork authorities but also to the whole audience. I did that in a big way, of course. I'm the one in the swirly patterned dress.

My second goal was to get higher access, respect, and closer friendship with the founder and CEO of eWomen-Network. I did that as well. She is a very humble woman who will do anything she can to help anyone feel better about herself and get further in business. I value our friendship very much and to this day can call on her for anything. I am just as accessible to her in return.

My third goal then became to maximize my experience on the trip, which I did. I ended up being a radio show guest on the Law of Attraction show on the Oprah and Friends XMRadio Network that weekend while I was there, which was totally unplanned. I also met a couple of Oprah's radio show and TV show producers and now have connections for future reference.

My goals that arose from this whole experience were to become a speaker at the eWomenNetwork annual conference the following year, which I did—twice. This opportunity also led to over $100,000 in revenue sales from clients who opted to work with me after seeing me at that event.

I also wanted to write my book and get it to the connections I made through my Oprah experience. I will be doing that this year, now that the book is finished.

But the best thing that happened from my big pay to play experience wasn't about earning more money or getting more exposure. It was about raising my confidence, expert status, and mindset, as well as internal shifts of what I felt capable of doing.

It truly was an experience of a lifetime. To view the videos taken of me bidding on stage or to read more about the experience, you can go to my blog archive at **http:// www.katrinasawa.com/category/oprah.**

However, my whole Oprah experience was just one way that I continue to pay to play. I also invest heavily every year in my own high-level mentor, someone who is making a lot more money than I am and who is doing the kinds of things I want to do.

I spend an average of $25,000 each year on my mentoring alone, not to mention business trips, workshops, paying my team, and contributing in other ways.

This is one of the most important things to notice, however, about yourself and your expectations. Are your expectations high but you're willingness low? Where are you investing, or where should you be?

Focus on your big vision

Like I mentioned before, I tend to go with my gut on many, if not all, of the decisions I make on investing, business or self-development, which new products or programs to launch, if I should take on someone as a client or not, and so much more.

I've learned along the way from various hand analysts, psychics, and intuitives that I've consulted that I have a gift of being able to manifest the things I want pretty quickly and easily.

I don't take that gift for granted, but I do tap into it every now and again. I think this is why I do tend to strongly believe that it will all work out in the end. I do get a lot of what I want. The only thing I didn't end up getting yet is the man of my dreams. Yes, I was married, but I was young, and it was before I grew into the woman I am now. I thought I found the right one a couple years ago. I'm not sure what happened there exactly, but God must have better things in store for me.

Granted, I haven't always moved as fast as I've wanted in my business. Looking back on it, though, it had to do with not staying focused on my big vision at all times.

I realize it can be tough constantly keeping your eye on the big prize when you have so much to do just to stay afloat. But it's true—it works.

Remember what that psychic told me in a reading before about being a trombone? That the Universe didn't know what I wanted.

The reason I had you develop your own big vision and vision board in the beginning of this journey was so that you can expand upon it as you go. You can see the possibilities arising and you can alter your vision accordingly.

Your big vision and goals will always evolve, you know; your big picture thinking will never end, if you don't let it, and that's a good thing. In order to be fully successful, you want to be constantly growing and reaching for more, serving and giving more, being more, and also loving yourself more, of course.

You need to fall in love with your purpose!

Your purpose has to be stronger than any fear.

Your purpose will establish your goals.

Your goals should scare you and excite you at the same time.

Your goals should inspire you to move to an increasingly higher level of awareness.

If you see how you're going to accomplish a goal, it's not a good goal; think bigger!

For example, if you know you can make $50,000 pretty easily in your business with your present results, then think bigger to what you can do if you plan for more. If you can see yourself making $75,000 this year, then you should plan for that, instead. But beyond that, aim for what you truly want. If you truly want to make $100,000, but you have no idea how you can get there, then that's your big, hairy goal, in my mind.

What you have to do, though, is start brainstorming how you CAN get there, not how you can't. What do you have to do to make it happen? Keep in mind that you will most likely need to be uncomfortable along the way. This is normal, however. Trust the process.

I urge you to make this a top priority. Keep your big vision on top of your mind at all times. Make sure those around you, who are your support structure, know your big vision too so they can encourage you to keep going, day after day.

Make sure that you set yourself up for success with daily reminders, checklists, rituals, or whatever you need to focus.

You never want to take your eye off the prize.

Asking for help

You are not alone, nor do you have to be alone in growing your business. I know sometimes it can be scary wondering where your next customer will come from, if the marketing will work, and if you will be able to pay your bills.

However, someone out there has done it before you. Someone out there has been in your shoes and succeeded. So don't feel like you have to reinvent the wheel.

I realize you're smart, sexy, and have a good head on your shoulders, but that doesn't mean you know how to successfully market and grow a company to six-plus-figure revenues, does it?

You might have to ask for help.

There's nothing wrong with that. I've asked for help, my mentors have asked for help, my friends and peers have all asked for help. My clients have also asked for help.

It just makes sense that to get further faster in your business, you ask someone who's been there, done that, and is where you want to be or close enough to it to help you get there.

The question is: Who can you trust, right?

Who is the perfect fit?

Who will steer you in the right direction?

Well, there's no exact science to it, unfortunately. I say go with your gut! That's what I did, and it's worked out pretty darn good for me.

Help can come in many forms, it can be:

- ❧ Technology support.
- ❧ Assistant and task-oriented support.
- ❧ Financial support.
- ❧ Of course, it can be in mentors you hire to show you how to do what they've done and inspire you to get there, too.

Technology is the easiest support to ask for. Just hire it. Don't try to understand too much of it, if it's not your forte.

Finding the right assistant is a little more challenging, because without some guidance in this area, you'll more than likely hire the wrong person for the wrong reasons or tasks in the beginning, like I did. Asking for referrals from trusted sources is the best way to find people to work for you and support you in your business. Realizing you may have to pay more for good talent is a hard pill to swallow, but keep in mind that you get what you pay for in business. Don't skimp on your support team.

Financial resources might be the biggest challenge of all for you, depending on your situation, family, support structure, and collateral. Most entrepreneurs I help launch and build their businesses don't end up needing business loans. They just need direction on how to invest the little money they do have wisely. Unfortunately, entrepreneurs often wait to ask for help and invest poorly based on their own knowledge. This depletes their reserves. When they realize their mistakes, it could be too late. They may not be able to find the funds they need to invest properly, causing them to struggle and go into the scarcity mindset.

One way to get around all that is to ask for help from the get-go; you'll end up making fewer mistakes and wasting less money and time in the process.

As for mentors, I choose people who:

- Stand out as being authentic with their message and their story.
- Are obviously making more money than I am and show it.
- Have already made many mistakes and learned from them, ensuring I can bypass that with their guidance.
- Have a specific and proven communication strategy and system.
- I trust, like, and connect with.
- Inspire me to think and play bigger.
- Can teach me things I still need to learn to grow and succeed even more.
- Are still in the trenches doing what it is that they teach.

"If I only knew then what I know now" is what we all say after one experience or another. I can clearly say that I would be a millionaire by now if I'd asked for help sooner in my entrepreneurial journey.

I thought I could figure it out myself. I figured, how hard could it be? I had the confidence (so I thought) to truly succeed.

But in looking back, I was so naïve.

ACTION STEP

Figure out where you're wasting time and energy, then repurpose that time and energy into more constructive activities that will allow you to change and/or reach your goals faster. Track your time for an entire week if you want to see where you spend your time and energy. It's amazing what this exercise does for you.

Determine where you may be able to systematize or automate more in your business. Who do you need to hire to help you? Assistants? Home help? Mentors?

Where should you be investing in your growth, learning, self-development, business planning, and implementation? It could be time to pay to play!

"Energy is the essence of life. Every day you decide how you're going to use it by knowing what you want and what it takes to reach that goal, and by maintaining focus."

⚮ Oprah

Chapter 12

Step Twelve—
From Inspiration to
Implementation

What does it mean to be an entrepreneur, and is this for you?

Not everyone is cut out to be an entrepreneur, in my mind. It takes so much determination, drive, and plain old guts to go out on your own in the world peddling your wares, selling yourself, and more.

It's definitely not for the faint of heart.

I believe that you know deep down inside if you're truly meant to be your own boss rather than work for someone else.

I know we all desire more freedom and flexibility in our lives and workdays, but that doesn't always mean you should be an entrepreneur. Really think about what this means.

Being an entrepreneur in my mind means to be:

- ❦ A creative thinker.
- ❦ Motivated almost all the time.
- ❦ A leader.

- ❧ In sales and marketing mode all the time.
- ❧ Financially focused.
- ❧ Led by purpose.

Does that describe you?

Do you have another way of looking at it, perhaps, which supports your decision in being an entrepreneur? If so, that's great; I'm happy for you.

Where to start

When developing your new business or transforming the business you have, we want to start with your inspiration. What inspires you? What is your bigger WHY, as we discussed earlier?

How does that play into your big vision of what you want your ultimate lifestyle to look like? How many hours did you want to end up working and with whom and how did you want to serve?

Then, once that is established, we can start building the right business for you.

I don't believe that you want to just go with whatever business opportunity is right in front of your face. There are too many supposed moneymaking schemes out there that lure you in and make you work ten times as hard as you have to just to make a few thousand bucks.

I'm talking about developing a business, from scratch, yet modeled after someone else doing something in a similar business structure.

You can make money from anything these days. Do you know that? Do you believe that?

Whatever your passion and purpose is, we can design a moneymaking business model around it and offer it in a way in which people will want to buy it for whatever price you want to charge for it. I truly believe this, and I've seen hundreds of examples of it over the last few years.

If you are already running your own business, there are so many other ways in which you can transform it into a more highly monetized, freedom-based, passion-driven, or leveraged business.

If you've just started your business or have been doing it for a short while now but can't figure out why you've hit a plateau at a certain level of income, hopefully you've got a better idea why that is by now. But if not, then there are ways for you, too, to restructure your business, your life, or your marketing to make it more profitable, I'm sure.

Putting together the right plan for where you want to take your business and how to get there is obviously a very important step. However, most entrepreneurs fail to complete this step. They often just set out to get clients by whatever means they can so they can start making money but with very little idea of how it will all come together.

The key is to design the business after the kind of lifestyle you want to have. There is a way to do that, and it happens when you choose the right business models to fit into your big picture.

Affordable, reliable options

You see, the traditional business models we were accustomed to seeing growing up are no longer the norm.

Traditional mom-and-pop establishments are still there, of course, but fewer and fewer are surviving.

Of course, many businesses flourish having a storefront location, such as a clothing or gift store, insurance company, restaurant, and electronics store.

There's nothing wrong with starting one of those types of businesses or a related business needing a storefront. In my experience, though, those take quite a bit of startup capital before you can even open your doors for business.

And you have set hours and expectations from the public as to when you'll be open and available, hence you'll be working a lot more or you'll have to hire employees, adding to the overall stress of running the business in the first place.

Those aren't the kinds of businesses I'm referring to or the ones I typically recommend that my clients start, although I've coached with many retail business owners.

There are much easier ways to make money, and you can do it on your terms, your hours, and in your way.

The businesses that I see are the most lucrative these days, and the ones that are really making money, are the services that focus on self-help or business growth and development. Makes sense doesn't it?

Why do you think I'm writing this book, *Love Yourself Successful*? It's designed to do both.

There are over fifteen different business models that I introduce to my coaching clients so they can choose which ones make sense for them to do.

Business models such as:

- 🌺 Online products like eBooks, CDs, home study programs
- 🌺 Video or webinar courses
- 🌺 Group mentoring or training programs
- 🌺 Monthly memberships
- 🌺 One-on-one coaching
- 🌺 Mastermind programs
- 🌺 Live events and workshops
- 🌺 Tele-classes and tele-seminars
- 🌺 Affiliate marketing
- 🌺 Becoming a published author
- 🌺 Speaking
- 🌺 Retreats
- 🌺 VIP days
- 🌺 Licensing or certification programs
- 🌺 Franchising
- 🌺 Advertising-focused websites, magazines, or email newsletters

I've done almost all of these at one point in my business. Having a variety of business models is one of the main reasons I'm making so much money. I'm more diversified.

Let's not get being diversified confused with being unfocused or frazzled by doing too many things. Because the only way I can do more than six of these at one time is because I have clear, implementable systems and a team of people to help me. There is no way I could do this much without those two things in place.

How did I learn how to have clear systems and the right team doing the right things to make this all happen? I had mentors who showed me what to do and I modeled after what they were doing to keep it simple.

Having a leveraged business with models like this is the key to having more freedom in your life, working the hours you want to work, making the money you want to make, and having the time off to spend with your kids, family, and take vacations. This is truly the way to love yourself successful; give yourself the gift of creating a proven, moneymaking business that will give you the ultimate lifestyle you desire.

Remember, you need to "do" certain things to become successful, but you also need to "be" as well. Focusing on both simultaneously is your best bet for success.

My final reminders to you:

- Learn to love yourself unconditionally.
- Stop settling for less than what you deserve or want.
- Think bigger than what you currently believe is possible.
- Have faith that it will all work out in the end.
- Never doubt that you can do something.
- Believe that there is an abundance of love and money out there and that you deserve as much as you want.
- Surround yourself with only positive, loving, and supportive people.
- Seek to find your happiest life ever and live BIG!

What's next?

Imagine you have the life that you want.

You have the man of your dreams who loves you for just who you are.

You love every bit of yourself too and feel completely hot and sexy every day.

Your cares are taken away because the money is flowing in so easily and effortlessly.

You have more time for yourself, your kids, your loved ones, your health and wellness, vacations, and more.

You have the luxury of being able to hire a housekeeper, landscaper, travel agent, personal assistant, and any other supportive person that you need.

You're giving and serving thousands of people with your gift and your message through your products and services.

The people you are serving are so overjoyed by working with you; they are receiving so much value.

You have reached the level of success that you knew you were meant to have.

This can all happen for you pretty quickly if you decide to take action and invest in yourself by learning how to do all this and then implementing it.

Inspiration is good, but without implementation, it's useless.

Don't become a statistic; become the reality of success you want to become and join the growing population of others who think like you do too.

ACTION STEP

To continue on your journey, try journaling every day. Record what you're grateful for each night before bedtime. Plot out your goals every year and each quarter and reach for bigger goals.

Go back to your original vision board and see what's missing or how much bigger you think now. Do you want more? Do you want to make more money? Enjoy more love and happiness in your life?

Stay connected with highly motivated, positive-thinking people who lift you up and encourage you to be your best self.

Seek the support and guidance you know can help you get to where you want to go in your life and your business and never give up. Remember, there are many resources and opportunities to take your learning and business development further at **www. LoveYourselfSuccessful.com/bookresources**. If you aren't completely sure what's possible for you or know all your options, I would love to talk with you in a complimentary business strategy session to help you figure that out. Go to **www.AskKat.biz** now to apply for a session with me and let's go!

Finally, love yourself successful and do whatever it takes for you to be completely happy!

About the Author

Katrina Sawa, The JumpStart Your Biz Coach

Katrina Sawa is an award-winning international Business Coach and Entrepreneur, the founder and CEO of K. Sawa Marketing International Inc., and the creator of The JumpStart Your Marketing® System and the Love & Money Business System.

Katrina is known as The JumpStart Your Biz Coach because she literally kicks her clients and their businesses into high gear. She works with highly motivated entrepreneurs who want to maximize and fast-track their businesses to make more money and enjoy more free time. Katrina uses online and offline Relationship Marketing systems and strategies to leverage your resources, contacts, and expertise; plus she kicks you in the butt to implement it all, too!

Katrina founded her business in 2002, and consistent networking and follow-up is the primary reason Katrina has been so successful.

Today she works with women primarily (and a few motivated, heart-centered men) to show them how to create freedom-based, passion-driven, moneymaking businesses so that they can live their happiest lives ever. She currently lives in the Sacramento, California area with her German Shepherd, Zeke.

With twenty-plus years' experience in sales, business, and marketing, plus a BS in Business, Marketing Concentration, Katrina speaks to groups of all sizes on how to start, build, grow, and market your business. Katrina has been featured on the Law of Attraction Show on the Oprah and Friends Radio Network as well as CBS and ABC news. Plus, she provides an abundant amount of free resources and information on her website at **www. JumpStartYourMarketing.com**.

As additional resources for you, since you invested in this book, Katrina has added a special hidden page on her website just for those of you who have bought the book. On that page, **www.LoveYourselfSuccessful.com/bookresources**, Katrina shares free downloads, an audio, and video for you, plus ways to get more information to take your Love & Money journey to the next level.

CPSIA information can be obtained
at www.ICGtesting.com
Printed in the USA
FSHW01n2201270418
47404FS